STREET GAMES

STREET GAMES

INSIDE STORIES OF THE
WALL STREET HUSTLE

ALAN LECHNER

HARPER & ROW, PUBLISHERS

NEW YORK

Cambridge
Hagerstown
Philadelphia
San Francisco

London
Mexico City
São Paulo
Sydney

1817

FIRST EDITION

Designer: Janice Stern

Library of Congress Cataloging in Publication Data

Lechner, Alan B
  Street games.
    1. Wall Street.   I. Title.
HG4572.L38 1980   332.64'273   79–2627
ISBN 0–06–012553–5

---

80 81 82 83 84 10 9 8 7 6 5 4 3 2 1

To Irv Levey

CONTENTS

ACKNOWLEDGMENTS

Nancy Cone, editor extraordinaire, mavin malgré elle. And all those Wall Streeters: the good ones for their help; the rest, without whom there would be no story.

INTRODUCTION: WHAT'S THE SCORE?

Wall Street is making a comeback. It was in trouble there for a while. It burned a lot of people. It burned them by giving a lot of bad advice. And advice is what it gives best.

It may seem strange to outsiders to see how well Wall Street survives. It goes down for the count, but always comes back stronger. And its customers keep coming back, too. Only they come back weaker. Wall Street survives because Americans love games. They love football and golf, they love Scrabble and charades, and "The Price Is Right." Most of all they love Monopoly.

Wall Street knows how people love to play games. That's its secret. It invents games, games for the public to play. The games are always fun, and they always hold out the promise that some day you may really own the Boardwalk.

Then the promise is broken and the game is over. Most people go home poorer. But that's when Wall Street gets busy. It knows that no one wants to play those old games again, so it's time to invent new ones. That's why the brokers and research departments are still there, discovering and inventing, trying to help customers forget the old games that didn't work out so well, and promising better luck next time. The financial institutions remain, too—the bank trust departments, the mutual funds, the pension fund advisers—bulging with the wealth of American and foreign savings that have become too mammoth to maneuver. Deep down they know they can't do the job well anymore. But they will never admit this to their clients, and they're only beginning to admit it to themselves.

This book is a kind of history of Wall Street in the 1970s. It's about Wall Street's search for a place in a rapidly changing investment world, and it's about the guy who made $4 million in Boeing options. It's also about the pharmacist who lost his shirt in a tax shelter he never paid enough taxes to need and the banks that dumped what they thought were soon to be worthless New York City bonds on unsuspecting customers at "bargain" prices. It's about those who championed the cause of the small investor—and the many more who didn't. It's about the great stock-market successes like Teledyne, Disney, and old AT&T; about the enormous failures perpetrated by the Cornfelds and Kings and their accounting masters of legerdemain who helped; and about the "Please call us or we'll call you" of a shrinking brokerage industry.

The 1960s proved that American streets were paved with gold. Throw a dart, buy a stock, watch your money double. The 1920s were here again. The sky was the limit. The professional money managers and advisers should have known it couldn't last, but they began to believe their own public relations. No cautionary words to customers, no suggestion of risk. Chicken Little be damned!

But then the sky did fall. From 1972 to 1974 the stock market tailspinned and crashed. Even the venerable Morgan Bank saw the value of its managed equity accounts drop some 50 percent. Pensions were no longer secure, and the individual fled the market with what little was left, vowing (as he had before) never to return.

If Wall Street had any conscience, it would have closed up shop and gone home. Had this been the Old West, bankers and brokers would have been pulled from behind their marbled pillars and run out of town on a rail. But Wall Street, reeling, still knew its customers. It knew that investment fever has always, eventually, overcome good sense.

The pros have learned how to excuse their errors: they invoke the will of the gods and absolve inconsistency by the constancy and similarity of their peers' mistakes. "Next time we shouldn't do it that way." "Had anyone realized it then." "No more investment trusts or mutual funds," say they. "But how about options or commodities or index funds or tax shelters? We know you didn't do so well in Avon when we recommended it at 140 and you sold it at 16. But how about Resorts International?"

Humility is a hard pill to swallow. So the game goes on. The players change, the names are different. But as long as the game might still make someone rich, it will have its participants. It's hard to tell how long it will last. Computers may soon make stockbrokers obsolete and many more brokers may be driving taxis; the Wall Street merger movement is accelerating, and negotiated commissions are making ever fewer firms profitable. For the first time Wall Street really needs the small investor, but some day even he may become cynical. Wall Street as we know it may be dying. But while it has any life left, it will struggle and fight to make us believe that this year's game is really new and only a fool wouldn't participate.

By last count there were some 25 million individual stockholders in the United States and another half million or so who make their living advising them. Many more millions have become investors through their pension fund contributions, and today those pension funds own more than one-fourth of all stock listed on the New York Stock Exchange.

This book gives an inside view of the games Wall Street plays. As in most street games, the biggest kids on the block make the rules. It's hard to win if you don't know the rules, and the guys on the street aren't telling. Without the rules, it's difficult to know where to stand when the game is Monkey in the Middle. Without the rules, playing Pin the Tail on the Donkey can make an ass out of anyone. It happens a lot when you play in the street.

Just knowing the rules may not be enough to guarantee a winning streak. But it sure improves the odds.

1

WHERE ARE THE CUSTOMERS' YACHTS?

In the good old days, before penicillin and polio vaccine, before helicopters and traffic jams, when people lit up Luckies and hardly anyone lived long enough to die of cancer, the Wall Street rich summered (as they still do) at the seashore—at Southampton, Westport, and Deal. Getting to the office was made somewhat less arduous by walking down the lawn to one's private motor yacht and cruising to the foot of Wall Street. The less fortunate sometimes hopped rides, becoming the precursors of modern-day car pools. But the less fortunate were few in the days of Prohibition and flappers.

The story goes that one day a gentleman and his stockbroker walked down Wall Street to the river, where they came upon the yacht lot. Upon inquiring, the gentleman was told that the yachts belonged to Wall Street brokers. "But where," he asked, "are the customers' yachts?"

The yachts are gone now, and the brokerage business is no longer the private club it once was. Senior partners use firm-owned helicopters to get to 8:30 A.M. office meetings. Junior partners remain in town during the summer and rent seats on the Friday seaplane to the Hamptons; many merely lease their summer beach houses. But stockbrokers as a group aren't hurting. Despite consolidations, mergers, and the advent of negotiated commissions, Wall Street is still a highly profitable business.

1

In the 1960s the growth of institutional business—the buying and selling of securities for bank trust departments, insurance companies, mutual funds, and pension funds—caused many firms to ignore the small customer. With commissions fixed by law, the institutions provided an enormous profit potential: while individuals might buy shares in the hundreds, institutions bought and sold in blocks of tens of thousands at the same commissions per share that we average investors paid.

When the institutions became big customers, the brokers doing business for them suddenly found themselves getting very rich on commissions. And the institutions knew it. They knew they had big bucks to give out (our bucks, to be sure) and they wanted all they could get in return. One thing they got was a new phenomenon on Wall Street: the institutional brokerage firm. These firms dealt only with institutional clients, and their big product was research. Huge staffs of highly paid security analysts were assembled by a new breed of firms with names like Donaldson, Lufkin and Jenrette; Faulkner Dawkins and Sullivan; and Auerbach, Pollack and Richardson. Most of them are gone now, the victims of negotiated commissions, but in their heyday they poured out 30-, 40-, and 80-page reports that analyzed the investment merits of a single corporation. Institutions liked this service. When the company's stock went up, the institution's investment officer looked good; when it went down, he had reams of paper to justify his bad investment decision.

For a while the Securities and Exchange Commission allowed the commissions to be split, at the direction of the institutions, between the firms which executed orders and those which provided services, usually research but occasionally of a less business-related nature. Sometimes large portions of the commissions paid by a client institution found their way back to some subsidiary or branch of that institution. Fee rebates were finally declared illegal by the SEC in 1968. Until that time the practice was widespread but no one was complaining. There was plenty to go around.

Wall Street was happy. Business was bigger than ever, bonuses were larger than ever. Some firms began to have paper-work problems because business was too good. Computers were on order to handle the load, and in the meantime the boys in the back office would just have to work overtime to deal with the mess. It turned out to be quite a mess for quite a while. Nothing serious—just things like not knowing which customers owned which stocks and how many millions of dollars worth of securities were either stolen or mistakenly discarded as trash. Well, those things would be taken care of.

The real problem was fixed commissions: brokers couldn't charge less for servicing customers even if they wanted to. It was the law of the Club, and the SEC backed it up. Not a bad deal, particularly in America, the land of free competition.

It took a lot of pressure to get the SEC to act, and commissions for the purchase and sale of securities finally became negotiable on May 1, 1975. As usual, Wall Street shrugged. The major firms had developed long-standing friendly relationships with institutional investment officers. So it would give gentlemanly discounts to its institutional customers; the retail customers' rates could be hiked to make up the difference. Few on Wall Street realized that institutions would soon come under close scrutiny by trustees, customers, and shareholders to insure that the cost of running money was reduced to a minimum.

Thus May 1, 1975, didn't quite arrive with the whimper that had been expected. Sure enough, institutions negotiated token discounts on small trades, and the brokerage firms were happy to comply. Then came the real trouble. Several member firms announced that they would cut rates drastically on all orders they transacted and that they would provide no other services—no expensive lunches, no theater tickets, no hotel suites, no research. May Day had indeed arrived. The pun was no longer a laughing matter. For years institutions had charged customers fees for using advertised expertise to manage customers' portfolios professionally. Institutions paid research staffs to analyze investment opportunities, but the average bank security analyst earned $15,000 a year. The real work was being done by the $50,000-a-year brokerage firm analyst (and superstars were being paid $100,000 plus). These guys were being supported by the fixed commission payments. Since such commissions were charged to customers' accounts, those commission payments never hurt institutional profitability; in fact, they helped to increase profits because institutions could avoid most of the research costs we thought they were incurring by hiring but not using those second-rate $15,000-a-year analysts.

Suddenly it became incumbent upon institutions to find the best price. While they knew that it might be years before the public figured out what was going on, they also knew that people like Abe Pomerantz were out there waiting. And no one wanted to deal with Abe.

Abraham Louis Pomerantz is a New York lawyer. Pomerantz' law firm long ago assumed the role of protecting the public in its dealings with the securities industry. If you are an investor, he may well be the best friend you've got.

Through the device of the minority stockholder (class action) suit, Pomerantz and his firm had already successfully pursued dozens of actions against mutual fund management companies that charged excessive fees and engaged in other fiduciary irregularities. The institutions knew that the commissions paid were just what Abe would want to look at. And they couldn't afford the publicity. (We'll get back to Pomerantz later.)

Within a relatively short period of time, commission discounts of up to 90 percent became commonplace on trades of large blocks of stock. Institutions may not have wanted to, but they *had* to bargain. Wall Street was distraught. The less profitable firms died, and those that remained scampered to retrieve the retail customers they had so recently disdained. Firms that once dealt only with institutions took down the "Retail customers need not apply" signs. The few firms that had steadfastly maintained and nurtured their retail clientele were besieged with offers to merge with, take over, buy out—anything—those once lofty institutional research houses. The small investor once again became a source of profit, one who was not expected to bargain for reduced commissions. What the small investor didn't know was that Wall Street needed him more than he needed the Street.

Now we're talking about power. Power to the people. You, the small investors, have waited a long time to get it. You have it now, though you may not realize it. You can demand and get more service, you can demand and get more information, you can demand and get lower commission rates; in some instances you may even be able to retrieve some past losses. You just have to learn how.

Someday stockbrokers as middlemen between buyers and sellers of securities may become obsolete. Someday we may be able to dial directly into some big IBM computer that will instantly find the buyer who will take the 100 shares of AT&T we want to sell. But until that day which brokers can't allow themselves to imagine, brokers will continue to live well on the fees they charge for transacting our orders.

It is the nature of stockbrokers to be optimistic. They like to believe that a rising market will continue to rise and that a falling market is about to turn. They need to think that. They make more money when the market goes up. You see, when the stock market falls, most investors are stuck. They didn't sell early enough. So they hold on. Holding on means no purchases, no sales, no commissions. If the market goes low enough, small investors finally give up. They sell—but they also go away. Wound-licking then takes time. And during that time whatever monies are left sit in savings banks or in Treasury bills. Brokers move out of sight and mind—at least until the next time cousin Fred starts bragging about all the money his broker is making for him in some new hot stock.

On the other hand, brokers make a lot of money when the stock market goes up. They suggest a purchase, you buy, they get their commission. The stock goes up. You make money. Good broker! The stock goes higher. The broker calls to say that while there may be some play left in XYZ Corporation, ABC is really beginning to move. You sell, you buy—commission once, commission twice. As you keep on buying stocks whose prices keep on rising, the process continues. The broker is really happy for you. He's glad you're making money. He's not a bad guy; he has an ego like everyone else. He looks good, and he likes it. He's also making a bundle. He may even complain to friends that the phone rings so often that he has to have lunch at his desk. Don't feel sorry for him. Brokers who have time for leisurely lunches don't take the seaplane to the Hamptons.

Wall Streeters should be seen as middlemen, as conduits between buyers and sellers of products. Were the Street to deal in oranges or shoes or the fish that are sold in the Fulton Street market nearby, hardly anyone would notice. But Wall Street's product is money. And money gives the street an aura and a respect that it often does not deserve.

There are two kinds of money that Wall Street deals with. The first is the money that the investor hopes to make; the second, derived from the first, is the money that brokerage firms earn by helping us participate in markets which may make us that first kind of money. Sometimes we make that money; more often we don't. But whatever the outcome, we pay Wall Street for the privilege of trying.

Today Wall Street's sorry that it didn't pay more attention to the individual investor. Each day brings new television and radio commercials aimed at him. Joan Fontaine tells us she's a member of the family at Lebenthal; everyone thanks Paine Webber; when E. F. Hutton speaks, Merrill Lynch's bull strolls down Wall Street. Those commercials cost money. Brokerage firms aren't hiring big-name advertising agencies because they have nothing better to do with their money. They're hiring those firms to get their message to the market they desperately want to reach. And that market is you.

So it's a new kind of buyers' market, a market that belongs to the individual. And one bit of leverage you now have is on commissions. Before May Day 1975 the commissions on institutional trades averaged 26 cents a share; by the end of 1977 they averaged 12 cents a share; today trades for as little as 3 cents a share are not uncommon. In what has become a highly competitive business, institutions have forced brokers who crave their business not only to bend but to fall to their knees. In 1976 the average rate of return on invested capital for all brokerage firms had been 18.5 percent. By 1977 that rate had fallen to 7.2 percent. At those levels of profitability most firms could have closed up shop. Something had to be done, and the small investor was the only bright spot on a gloomy horizon.

If May Day served to reduce commissions for institutions, it was also the time to increase rates for the small investor. Retail rates increased an average 3 to 4 percent in 1975. Merrill Lynch is understood to have raised its retail rates that year an average of 6 to 8 percent to establish a higher base from which its more active "sophisticated" retail customers might negotiate some modest discount. In January 1978 Merrill Lynch announced a further 7 to 8 percent increase on retail commissions, and most firms followed its lead. Still another commission increase for small investors was instituted by several firms in January 1979. As institutional rates kept falling, retail rates kept rising. Yet brokers seem to know what they are doing; despite a grand jury impaneled in 1976 to investigate the retail rate increases (the jury is still out), there has been little outcry from the retail public, which as a whole seems to be insensitive to commission rates.

Next time you speak to your broker, you might ask about commission discounts. He'll probably fall off his chair, particularly if you're the kind of customer who speaks to him more than twice a year. He may tell you that his firm doesn't do that sort of thing. Tell him you know other firms. If he starts to stammer, tell him about your aunt who doesn't trade any more than you do but gets a 25 percent discount from her broker at (if you're talking to Merrill Lynch, say Blyth Eastman Dillon; if you're talking to Bache, say—you know what I mean). If you still get no positive response, ask about the discount brokers. He'll tell you that they won't give you any service, but he probably doesn't give you much himself anyway. Now don't try any of these ploys if your participation in the market amounts to adding one share of Coca-Cola to your portfolio each Ground Hog Day. If you maintain any reasonably active account, however, you should not be paying full commissions. And don't let your broker get away with saying he has to check firm policy. All Wall Street firms discount, and—within reason—your broker can make that decision for himself.

Commission discounts won't make up for poor stock selection, but in these days of bargain air fares to Europe, a 25 percent commission discount on moderately active accounts could get you and a friend two round-trip tickets.

Wall Streeters may wear pinstripe suits and Gucci loafers, but they are nevertheless just like the rest of us, all out there trying to make a living. Most of them will be accommodating if you ask for help (or a commission reduction), but there's no reason, so far as they are concerned, to force discounts on an unknowing or undemanding public. Commission discounts aside, most brokers are scrupulously honest and will give advice to the best of their often limited abilities. I've seen many turn away orders when they thought a customer was embarking on a mistake. Most develop caring, paternal attitudes toward those they number among their naive clientele. But, as in any business, there are others. Forewarned is forearmed.

One day a few years ago John Lawrence phoned. He is a professor of English literature at an Ivy League college, and we have a lot in common: he understands the intricacies of the stock market as well as I understand Coleridge's dream theory. John was calling about his mother, Dorothy Lawrence, then in her seventies. She had never had much money, but sometime after World War II she had bought some stock in Eastman Kodak. Dorothy was not exactly a broker's dream client. She had put the Kodak stock away and every now and again received notices of stock splits and stock dividends. She had signed some papers instructing the company to buy additional shares with whatever cash dividends were paid, and by 1973 her original $10,000 investment had increased twelvefold without her ever incurring the cost of another broker's commission. Dorothy wasn't rich, but she didn't live rich either. With Social Security, a small insurance annuity, and a rent-controlled apartment she could get by nicely. And she had her Kodak bankroll for her old age.

In 1973 Dorothy didn't worry much about money. She was waiting for a grandchild. But John read the newspapers, and to him things didn't look right. He told me what his mother held, and he asked for advice. I advised him to tell her to tell a broker to sell everything. It seems that in 1973 everyone but Wall Street, everyone including professors who taught nineteenth-century British poetry, knew that something was wrong. In fact it wasn't hard to see: Nixon was in trouble with the economy, inflation had gone into double digits, and wage and price controls weren't working. The Vietnam War was ending, and the boys would be coming home to an overheated economy that would now have to curtail war production; there would be no jobs for them or for the people at Boeing, Lockheed, and DuPont who had been added to late shifts to pour out fighter planes, Napalm, and bombs. And interest rates were at historic levels. Who needed stocks when bonds were paying up to 10 percent and were still climbing? The stock market looks to the future, and in 1973 only the past looked good.

Two months later I heard from John again. His mother hadn't sold anything. The $120,000 was down to $80,000. What to do now? I told John to have his mother come to see me. This time I'd charge her when I told her to sell.

In 1973 I had been out of Wall Street for three years. When I retired to the academic life in 1970, all my blue suits and french-cuffed shirts had gone into mothballs. I had the feeling, however, that the confidence I hoped to inspire in Mrs. Lawrence would not be helped by my present image of baggy tweeds, so I dusted off a pinstripe and put on a tie. I knew that my hair was a shade long by Wall Street standards, but after all I was known to be a college professor and some leeway would have to be allowed.

Dorothy arrived filled with apologies. She still didn't care much about the money, but she felt she had been naughty and disrespectful. She promised to be good and to do whatever I suggested. We drank sherry and discussed fees. I had suddenly become a professional investment adviser again; my retirement to the academic life had ended.

I told Dorothy that I thought the market would continue to fall and that her Kodak should be sold. Fine, she said, but what about her other stock?

"What other stock?" I asked, a little too loud. "John just said Kodak." Dorothy, head bowed, refusing to look at me, handed over a slip of paper. In very neat columns headed Company, Number of Shares, Purchase Price, and Date of Purchase her holdings were listed.

Eastman Kodak	1,076 shares
Syntex	100 shares
McCulloch Oil	100 shares

Syntex and McCulloch, two of the hottest, most volatile stocks in that market! Where had they come from, and what the hell were they doing in this little old lady's portfolio?

Dorothy explained that when John transmitted my original instructions, she called her broker at one of Wall Street's better-known firms to ask his advice. Dorothy wasn't one of their better-known customers; in fact she hadn't made a trade in nearly twenty years. The telephone operator didn't recognize the name Dorothy asked for, and after some checking it was discovered that her broker had died five years before. (Starvation perhaps.) Sure enough, Dorothy was still on the books. They put her through to some young man who had taken over the deceased's accounts, and she asked him about selling.

He didn't agree. "Not the right time," he said. But as long as she was on the phone, how about a little diversification? He thought her portfolio was too heavy in Kodak, and his firm was really bullish on Syntex and McCulloch Oil. He told her that lots of people liked those stocks and that Dorothy could make some quick bucks. Dorothy demurred. Not one to make quick decisions, she said that she didn't think that kind of stock was for her. She forgot about selling, now wanting only to get off the phone. The bright young man suggested that she think about it.

She hung up and forgot about it—until the young man called ten days later. "Mrs. Lawrence," he said, "about Syntex and McCulloch. Should have listened to me. Both up. Don't you want to see your portfolio grow? There's still time. How about 100 of each?"

"He sounded like such a bright young man," she told me, "so I said O.K."

I looked at the slip of paper. In less than a month Dorothy had dropped more than $4,000 in those two stocks alone. $4,000! That's a year of Social Security checks for a woman who makes sure she gets on buses before 5 P.M. in order to pay 25 cents instead of 50 cents. I tried to remain calm. I'd seen Wall Street do this to people before, and that was one of the reasons I had gotten out—not enough customers' yachts!

Dorothy was perplexed when I asked for the authority at least to get back her losses in those two hot stocks. I went into a long dissertation on the "know your customer" rule.

Rule 405 of the New York Stock Exchange, under the heading "Diligence as to Accounts," requires brokers to learn all they can about their customers and, with that information, to protect their customers from acting in ways that may be detrimental to the customers' own best interests. Of course, brokers can't force determined investors *not* to sell short, buy commodity futures, or sell naked options. But brokers must inform customers that certain transactions may not be suited to their portfolios. And they must carefully explain why. If one of the Rockefellers wants to take 10 percent of his portfolio and play around in penny stocks or this year's latest craze, that's fine. But you don't sell tax-free municipal bonds to someone who doesn't pay enough taxes to make those bonds economically worthwhile; you don't take orders from minors; you don't offer Resorts International to a retired person who is getting along nicely on the dividends from a portfolio of AT&T, Georgia Power and Light, or Rochester Gas and Electric. And you don't offer Syntex and McCulloch Oil to Dorothy Lawrence.

People like Dorothy fall into the category of naive investors.

The New York Stock Exchange has mandated that these people be protected, usually from themselves. In Dorothy's case, had she initiated the request to the broker for the purchase of the two stocks, it would have been the broker's responsibility to question her motives and to explain carefully, after reviewing her account, why those stocks were not appropriate for someone in her age and income bracket. Her fooling-around years had long since passed. If she wanted action Atlantic City Electric was as close to the casinos as she should get. The rule goes further: most brokers interpret it to mean that when someone like Dorothy insists, the broker should bring in a managing partner to try further to convince her of her folly. After that, the responsibility would become Dorothy's.

But in the case in question, Dorothy had been a sitting duck.

I explained the rule to her, but she insisted that it was her fault. She didn't have to buy the stock. It's hard to convince an otherwise sane woman that she had not been responsible for her action. When I told her she could get her $4,000 back, she brightened a little. I explained that it would take only one phone call to the senior partner of the firm involved. I speculated that I'd get through to his secretary, who would dutifully inquire as to the nature of my call. Then I would explain that I thought it polite to inform the partner of the actions of one of his employees *before* I called the New York Stock Exchange. I told Dorothy that it was likely, in light of Dorothy's particular circumstances, that the partner would come on, ask the exact dollar amount of the losses, write a check, and fire the account executive.

That's where I made my mistake. Dorothy didn't want anyone to get in trouble. The young man sounded so sweet; maybe he had a family. For what was probably no more than $100 in commissions, this sweet young man had screwed Dorothy out of $4,000—and she was feeling sorry for him! Besides, her brother-in-law did business with the firm, and maybe he wouldn't like it if Dorothy caused trouble. Dorothy, scrupulously nice, wouldn't protect herself. The case was closed. I saw her out.

We did take Dorothy's account to another firm, but that young man is probably still with the old firm, doing the same thing to lots of Dorothys who don't have the sense or the indignation to protest. Most brokers don't act this way. But enough do, and only we can do something about them.

Abram Chasins did do something about them. Chasins is the retired music director of the New York Times radio stations, a well-known musicologist, author, and composer who has spent most of his life doing research. People like Chasins get to use their noses a lot, and their noses come to tell them when things smell right and when they smell fishy.

In 1970 something smelled fishy. Smith, Barney & Co. was a sponsor of one of Chasins' programs on WQXR. Not surprisingly, Abram got to know some of Smith Barney's people and opened an account with the firm. During the year he bought stock, valued at $34,950, in various corporations recommended by the firm. These securities, traded over-the-counter, soon went south. Abram sold out for $16,333.

Stocks traded over-the-counter are usually those of companies that are not large enough to be listed on an organized security market like the New York, American, or Pacific stock exchanges. Rather than being sold at auction on a stock exchange, as are the securities of listed companies, these securities are marketed by various brokerage firms. When a customer places an order to buy such securities, those firms often sell directly from their own inventories; when a customer sells, the firms themselves often buy the securities to add to their own inventories. Unlike ordinary brokerage services (the finding of a buyer for a seller and a seller for a buyer, for which activities the broker earns a commission), over-the-counter trades are transacted net; that is, the dealer simply offers to buy at one price and offers to sell, if possible, at a higher price. The dealer's profit comes from the spread—the difference between the buy and sell (the bid and asked) prices.

Thus, when Chasins bought the securities that Smith Barney recommended, he was buying not from some anonymous seller out there in investor land but from Smith Barney itself. And nobody told him. Abram is no Dorothy. When he found out, he called his lawyer. Smith Barney doesn't need clients like Chasins. The courts ruled that proper disclosure had not taken place, and Smith Barney was ordered to reimburse Chasins' losses plus interest. Smith Barney no longer sponsors programs on WQXR, and Abram Chasins no longer gives his brokerage business to Smith Barney.

Smith Barney may not have been doing anything that was morally wrong when it offered securities to Chasins. It may well have believed that the securities in question would increase in value. Nevertheless, as a result of the Chasins case, when brokers now "make markets" in the securities that their customers buy, the confirmation slip that the customer receives clearly states, "We make a market in this issue." Abram Chasins took away from investors an opportunity to get even with stockbrokers who may try to dump their inventory on the public, but in so doing he made security trading a little bit safer for all of us.

A few years ago the "know your customer" rule hit one brokerage house where it hurt. A broker received a call from a sophisticated-sounding chap who asked about opening an account. He also asked some penetrating questions about a number of currently hot stocks. The papers for opening the account were duly sent and returned, and the customer, as yet unmet, phoned in an order for a reasonable number of shares in one corporation. The shares were bought and should have been paid for within five business days. But before that period had elapsed the customer phoned in an order to sell the shares—at a profit. Normal procedure requires that a customer, even in these circumstances, mail or deliver a check covering the cost of his purchase before the brokerage firm credits his account with the difference between the two transactions. But sometimes rules are skirted and, after all, there was a profit. The customer was on his way.

Over the next eighteen months the customer's trades grew in size, and so did his profits. And not once did he put up a dime. The broker was doing well on commissions—the guy was a smart, active trader—and the broker thought he didn't have a care. The customer kept extending himself, always heavily margined.

Buying on margin means borrowing money from the brokerage firm for the purchase of securities; the actual amount is based on the market value of the account. It is an accepted Wall Street practice and is regulated by the Federal Reserve Board. (At the time of this writing, customers with at least $2,000 in their accounts can borrow, usually at one percent above the prime rate, up to 50 percent of the costs of the stocks they purchase.) This customer's account grew to close to $1 million in value.

Then another bull market burst. Securities prices tumbled. The broker began calling the customer, asking him to put up more money. (More money? Remember, he had never sent any!) He said a check would be in the mail. Security prices continued to fall, and the broker should have sold him out long before the value of the stocks held fell below the amount owed to the brokerage firm. But he was such a good customer! With no check forthcoming, the stocks were finally sold, with the firm out a fair amount of change on those margin loans. Naturally, the firm went after the customer. And it found him. In flagrant violation of the "know your customer" rule, the high-flying trader turned out to be a seventeen-year-old college freshman who thought it might be fun to dabble in the market. Under the law—civil, criminal, and administrative—the kid was a minor, an infant. His family might have been responsible were it not for rule 405. The broker never got to know his customer. He got fired instead.

An extreme working of the "know your customer" rule occurred a few years back. Harry Winston walked into the Miami office of a New York brokerage firm, opened an account, and bought 20 options on Zenith (each option contract covered 100 shares of Zenith common stock). The next day he returned to buy 20 options on Xerox. The rules say that you must pay for any purchase within five business days. Mr. Winston said he was off to New York and would present a check to the main office.

His name preceded him. On his arrival at the New York office, Mr. Winston found the carpet laid, and he was greeted with appropriate pomp by the partner in charge. No matter that he had mistakenly carried the wrong checkbook. So many different banks to deal with, so hard to remember which account was full and which one was used only for petty cash. He'd stop by or send someone the next day with the funds.

Mr. Winston and the partner drank coffee from the china cups that each firm reserves for visiting royalty. Small talk ensued.

The partner, somewhat shy about intruding on his captive audience, wondered gently whether he might ask Mr. Winston for some professional advice. His wife's birthday was a week away. An emerald would be nice; might he buy one through Mr. Winston for, say, $5,000? Mr. Winston smiled in that fatherly manner reserved for the naive child and apologized. Certainly, another jeweler might have an inferior stone in that price range, but his clientele wouldn't tolerate such an offering. The partner knew a put-down when he heard one, but he recovered nicely by protesting his innocence and suggesting that perhaps $10,000 would do justice to his wife. The lesson had been learned. Mr. Winston agreed that a lovely stone could be had at that price. He would select it himself and instruct its delivery the following day.

The partner reached for his checkbook. Mr. Winston protested; surely inspection should precede payment. The partner would hear none of it. If Mr. Winston was selecting, that was good enough for him. He wrote the check: *Pay to the order of Harry Winston $10,000.* Mr. Winston deferred, neatly folded the check, tucked it into his Gucci billfold, and disappeared forever. You see, Harry Winston *was* Harry Winston; he just wasn't *the* Harry Winston.

As if stockbrokers didn't have enough problems, a new bombshell exploded in December 1978. If appeals don't mitigate its force, it may keep on exploding for years to come. For what may be the first time, the courts have held that brokerage firms may be liable for the results of actions they recommend. And one such recommendation may now cost the firm of Blyth Eastman Dillon more than $1 million.

The story, which seems to be on its way to making history, began ten years ago. In March 1969 Dr. David Rolf, an Ohio opthalmologist, had an account at Eastman Dillon, Union Securities (the firm had not yet merged with Blyth & Co.). The account was handled by his broker on a discretionary basis; that is, the broker had the authority to buy and sell for the account without receiving permission for each trade from the client. Then Dr. Rolf's broker left the firm. The account was taken over by one Michael Stott, another broker at the firm. Mr. Stott did not have or want the discretionary authority of his predecessor, and he suggested that Dr. Rolf hire an independent investment adviser. Dr. Rolf requested suggestions, and Mr. Stott provided two names. One was Akiyoshi Yamada, a hot young star of the late 1960s. In May 1969 Dr. Rolf signed on.

When Mr. Yamada got the account, he began selling off Dr. Rolf's high-quality securities, replacing them with more speculative stocks. Dr. Rolf began to worry, and he told this to Mr. Stott, who still acted as the account's overseer. Stott told him not to worry. From May 1969 to March 1970 the value of Dr. Rolf's portfolio dropped from $1.4 million to $446,000. Dr. Rolf was worried. But not as worried as Stott should have been.

In 1970 it was discovered that Yamada was a swindler who was using clients' money to manipulate stocks for his own gain. He was convicted of fraud and sent to prison. Dr. Rolf filed suit against Blyth and Stott, charging them with fraud. He claimed that Stott had given him very costly advice.

An initial court action awarded Dr. Rolf $55,790 in damages. Not nearly enough, thought he, and in 1977 he appealed. An appellate court upheld Dr. Rolf's assertion and ordered Blyth Eastman Dillon to pay damages that could run to over $1 million. Blyth is trying to take its case to the Supreme Court. Whether or not the Court hears the case, the public's naive belief that brokers (and bankers, mutual funds, and pension funds managers) are fiduciaries (from the Latin *fides,* trust) who are responsible for the advice they give, soon may be legally enforced.

Someday if a bank trust officer tells you that your portfolio decreased by 50 percent in the previous year, you may have more recourse than the removal of your account. At the very least, you may not have to pay his fee for his less than exemplary performance. Someday brokers may have to take some credit for their costly "suggestions"—and not just their commission credit. Someday it may not be enough to say, "We were wrong." But until that day comes, you are fair game. Now, more than ever, you are where the commission bucks are—the bucks that go along with stocks and bonds, options and commodities, funds and tax shelters. Sometimes the "know your customer" rule doesn't apply or is skirted. Sometimes you're not made quite aware of what you're buying or risking, as you deserve to be. Sometimes you have recourse, but not often.

So you're the most popular kid on the block. How you got that way is a story in itself.

2

THE PUBLIC NEED
NOT APPLY

Groucho Marx was fond of saying that any club that would take him wasn't worth joining.

When Wall Street talks about the Club, it's not the Stork or the Racquet or the River. It's the New York Stock Exchange itself. In the old days, before 1960, they might not have taken Groucho; today it might not be worth joining.

The Club was organized in 1792 by a group of brokers who bought and sold public stock, in those days primarily Revolutionary War scrip. They met, rumor has it, under an old buttonwood tree and made a pact: no member of the Club would transact business for the public at *less* than a specified rate, and each member would give all others preferential treatment.

For 183 years the New York Stock Exchange stuck to those rules. Until the fateful May Day 1975, the NYSE was the only private business organization in America legally operating as a cartel that could fix prices against the public interest. So entrenched was the Exchange in American history that when the securities laws were written in 1933 and 1934, the Exchange was continued as an organization that would regulate itself and be allowed to continue pricing practices that in any other enterprise would constitute gross restraint of trade. But nobody, not even the SEC, would mess with the Club.

The Club held the corporate and securities world by the short hairs. Any major company that wanted widespread distribution of its stock and the maintenance of a continuous trading market for that stock eventually had to list its shares on the NYSE. And any investor who wanted to purchase or sell those securities had to do so through members of the Club—at whatever commission rates those members charged for doing your business for you.

The Club was organized officially as a "not for profit institution," which may be the biggest semantic joke of all time. True, the NYSE is not a profit-making organization. But its members are! And with commissions fixed at extortionately high levels, its members profited as perhaps no other group in modern times. Were it not for its members' own greed, their infighting, and their utter unwillingness to adjust to the modern age, it might still continue to enjoy that position. The Club is now on the verge of drowning, and no one knows how much longer it will manage to keep afloat. If we're not careful, it could take us down with it.

The members of the Club, the 1,366 individuals who own "seats" on the New York Stock Exchange, break down naturally into two groups, the upstairs firms and the floor traders. The upstairs members are the ones we know best; among them are Merrill Lynch; Bache; Smith Barney; Bear, Stearns; E. F. Hutton. They are the brokers with whom we transact our securities business. The second group, the floor traders, are primarily smaller firms or individuals who as members trade their own accounts, act as specialists for particular stocks, or handle overflow business for either the larger firms or nonmembers.

Public relations hyperbole notwithstanding, the members of the Club were there for their own self-interest. And when the interests of members conflicted with the interests of their investing customers, the members usually considered themselves first. That would be perfectly acceptable if the public could take its business elsewhere—that's what free enterprise is all about—but Wall Street runs only one way. The Club was a cartel, a government-protected monopoly. You played the game their way or not at all. In a strictly legal sense, the SEC had jurisdiction over the NYSE. But the principle of self-regulation was so deeply entrenched that the SEC would require changes in operations only after going through tedious processes that involved suggestions, hearings, and sundry legal maneuvers.

The Club functioned smoothly well into the 1950s. Then the first cracks appeared, almost imperceptible fissures, barely visible to the naked I (as in Investor). Those fissures were caused by the growth of mutual funds.

The mutual funds—Dreyfus, Fidelity, Oppenheimer, and the lot—came to control billions of investment dollars, dollars that the public subscribed for investment in common stocks. The Club was smart; it strictly proscribed mutual funds as members. If the funds wanted to buy common stocks, they would have to do so like everyone else through member brokers. But the funds were smart, too. They could add. Since the Exchange made no provisions for commission discounts to big customers, the mutual funds added up the millions that their business was bringing to Club members. Nobody gets that kind of money for nothing. The mutual funds asked their friendly neighborhood brokers for something in return. It didn't take the brokers long to realize that if they didn't put out, someone else would.

It was a bit like the familiar story of the woman who was asked if she'd sleep with the King of England for $1 million. "Of course," she said. "Would you sleep with me for $10?" asked the interrogator. Indignantly, she asked just what kind of girl he thought she was. "We already know that," he replied. "We're just down to negotiating a price."

For what you and I, individually, have to offer, Wall Street can afford the highest pretense of morality. But the mutual funds were a different ballgame. The funds paced their demands. What they asked at first seemed relatively simple. If brokers were to enjoy the funds' commission business, then brokers in return were asked to use their best efforts to find customers to subscribe to the mutual funds. Once the word got out, the big funds sat back and enjoyed the scramble. Brokers fell over each other trying to satisfy the funds—and, coincidentally, to increase their own commission business. It was like a sweepstakes with the funds keeping score. The good brokers—good at hustling the funds—did well. And the funds grew larger the easy way.

Notice, if you will, that although commission discounts had not yet arrived, a kind of payment for commission business had begun. It would be a while before anyone bothered to notice that the clout of mutual fund *shareholder* money was being used not in the shareholders' interest but rather to increase the number of shareholders, thereby increasing the total dollar amount of the fund (and, of course, the fees that went to the fund managers, who were paid a percentage of the now larger fund's assets).

History will probably record that the biggest mistake the Club made was to allow this first "extra" service for large customers. For nearly two hundred years no extra had been given by any member to any customer. When the first member gave that extra service, the Club could have stopped it with a word. Such was the power the Club exercised over its members. But the Club chose to look the other way; or perhaps it didn't bother to notice at all.

Once the Club had given that first inch, the structure began to weaken. Like sharks smelling blood, the funds knew they could play off one greedy member against another. As the funds grew so did the commissions they generated. And so did their demands.

What they demanded was called, appropriately, the give-up. And that's where the real trouble started.

Just as many brokers who were members of the NYSE found new customers for the mutual funds, thousands of other brokers who were not members of the Club (usually smaller firms throughout the country and members of such regional exchanges as the Boston, Midwest, and American stock exchanges) were sending a lot of new clients to the funds. The funds could not compensate these brokers for their services by placing commission business with them. Mutual funds concentrated their purchases in stocks listed on the NYSE, and nonmembers could not trade there. So one day, somewhere, someone thought up the give-up.

It worked like this: An institution would place a normal order with a member of the Club, and a normal commission would be paid. But the member broker was instructed by the institution to send a check, perhaps for 50 percent of the commission payment, to a nonmember broker as a token of the fund's appreciation for services rendered. I wonder who claims credit for thinking up the idea. Whether it was a fund manager or a member broker, the idea was one whose time had come, and it took off like a bat out of hell. And why not? Brokers were getting so damned rich on institution business that they could give away much more than half and still be sitting pretty.

Soon the bank trust departments, the insurance companies, the pension fund managers had joined in the give-up game. They too had large commissions to hand out, and they found give-ups a convenient way to settle certain debts without actually paying for them. Wall Street was now a de facto discounter. It sent the give-up checks where it was told and usually asked no questions. Unfortunately, sometimes the give-up went right back to the fund—not to the shareholder, but to its manager (or to his bank in the Bahamas). And that was just too much, even for the Securities and Exchange Commission. After all, there are limits. What you do in the privacy of your own boardroom is one thing; exposing yourself in public is going too far.

There had always been a very close relationship between the New York Stock Exchange and the SEC. Many SEC commissioners and employees eventually left government service to find highly lucrative positions with firms that just happened to be NYSE members. But a distant roar was beginning to be heard from Washington. In April 1968 the Justice Department, which did not yet have the power to deal with the securities markets, began to formally question the validity of fixed brokerage commissions. Probably to keep Justice (is that a capital or small j?) from moving in on its turf, the SEC (again, later rather than earlier) banned the give-up in December

1968. At the same time it suggested that a volume discount of up to 40 percent could be given on all trades of over 1,000 shares.

The Club thought it had won a victory. Its members were glad to trade in the give-up for those supposed discounts. The net effect in dollars and cents meant millions added to member firms' profitability. Somehow they missed seeing that the cracks were growing bigger. The SEC itself was now standing on trembling, if not shaky, ground. It had outlawed sharing, but it had called for discounting while still preserving price fixing. What was against the law for one group (i.e., the rest of the corporate world) had been reinforced for another. Sure sounds like favoritism. Or job hunting? Or was the Club as a whole perhaps a big political contributor? Whatever it was, the law still didn't want to mess with it.

While the institutions had lost the give-up, they still had their "soft dollars." Soft dollars are very special. They bear no resemblance to such hard currencies as the German mark, the Swiss franc, and the Japanese yen; they have nothing to do with Russian rubles or Polish zloty. They are a legal tender unto themselves, and they can buy almost anything. But only financial institutions can spend them, and only on Wall Street.

Before the advent of commission discounting, the NYSE constitution mandated that commissions were to be fixed at the prevailing level "and shall be net and free of any rebate, return, discount or allowance made in any shape or manner, or by any method or arrangement direct or indirect." The language seems pretty clear. Do you get the impression that it applies only to cash? Does it seem to indicate that you can give away your house, your hotel, or your mother? Or that you can let your employees work for your customers free of charge?

Well, that's how Wall Street, the Club and its members, interpreted the constitution. In return for institutional commission business, the Street felt perfectly free to give those customers any service (or almost any service) that those customers might demand. The Street, forbidden price competition, went wild on "service" competition. Since service usually meant research, this gave rise to the institutional research brokerage firm. These firms, members of the NYSE, accepted only institutional accounts. Their principal product was in-depth research reports on the companies that institutions wanted to know about. And any institution could get on their mailing list—at a cost: a minimum of $10,000 a year in commissions on the trades that the "research" firm would transact for the client institution.

That's why they were soft dollars, "soft" because the institutions weren't using their own money or revenues. The commissions were charged to the accounts of customers who kept their money in mutual funds, bank trust accounts, or pension funds.

Soft-dollar payments went not only for the brokerage firm's standard product. If you were a mutual fund manager who wanted to know about a company not followed by the research firm, the firm would be more than happy to have some ace security analyst find out whatever you wanted to know about it. But you would have to pay extra for the service, perhaps $5,000 in cash or, if you preferred, an additional $15,000 in commissions (soft dollars were usually charged at a 3:1 ratio to the real stuff). As the soft-dollar derby grew, the list of available services also grew. A soft $25,000 might buy a detailed study of trade possibilities with China; $2,000 soft, a weekly computer tabulation of the relative performance of 500 mutual funds. Brokerage firms posted the available services and their soft-dollar prices. No one seemed to think the practice violated the fixed-commission statute.

There were two major problems with the soft-dollar arrangement.

1. Where they provided services necessary to the better management of institutional monies, they served a definite investment purpose. But the institutions were charging their customers, through management fees, for those services. Since the institutions were in fact getting the services "free," how about lowering the fees charged to the customers? You didn't see many headlines announcing reductions. Rather, the customers continued to be billed as though the managers were hiring

and paying for all that super research. And all the while most institutions kept what amounted to skeletal staffs while the managers pocketed the extra change.

2. While there was an accepted, publicly offered market basket of services that institutions could choose to dip into, there was also a second string of services available for those much-sought soft dollars. Only no one talked openly about that list, and nobody ever got to see it as such. On it were theater tickets, dinners at expensive restaurants ("Charge it to the broker's account when you leave"), hotel suites that just happened to be vacant when some bigwig arrived, girls who just happened to drop into the suites, airline tickets to no convention in particular, and limousines to save the tired fund manager the exertion of hailing a cab after a night at Regines.

Soft dollars bought a lot of nice things. At the same time, they highlighted the fiction of fixed commissions. If brokers could spend so much to satisfy their customers (here I'm speaking only of the cost of what were deemed to be legal soft-dollar services), couldn't they eliminate the services and lower the fixed commissions? A lot of people saw what was going on, and they started asking just this sort of question.

When the give-up had been banned and soft-dollar payments became questionable, the mutual funds didn't lie down and play dead. They decided to attack. If the Club wouldn't give up to them what they had come to expect, they would try a new wedge. Why not join the Club and beat it at its own game? A number of big institutions, primarily mutual funds, set up brokerage firm subsidiaries to apply for NYSE membership.

Since 1968 nearly 60 institutions had become members of regional exchanges. Where those exchanges jointly listed companies with the NYSE the institutions were able to have all the commission dollars revert to themselves. The ethical among them passed those savings on to their shareholders; the less moral became richer. The problem, however, was that not enough NYSE issues were listed on the regional exchanges. The institutions still had to do most of their business through members of the Club, and they didn't like it a bit.

In 1971 the Dreyfus Corporation, through a brokerage affiliate, applied for NYSE membership. Its application was quickly followed by that of Jeffries & Company, a subsidiary of Investors Diversified Services, the largest mutual fund complex in the United States. Rumors abounded concerning who would be next and what the NYSE would do about it.

The Exchange had a problem. It had rules that denied admission to publicly held corporations, and it tried to apply those rules to the brokerage subsidiaries. Nothing against them personally, of course; it was just that the institutions (including banks, which no one expected would try to join because of banking laws) were paying NYSE members a few hundred million dollars a year. If those customers became members, the present members would lose customers. Robert Haack, who became president of the Exchange in 1967, had gotten himself fired by publicly proclaiming in 1970, in a speech to the Economics Club (1,200 of this country's business and financial leaders), that "the vestiges of the private club atmosphere which remain at the New York Stock Exchange must be discarded." He explained that fixed commissions, which brought the industry revenues of $3 billion, also brought the industry the scandal of reciprocal relationships and kickbacks.

It made no difference. The Exchange, self-protective as ever, denied membership to institutions. And the SEC went along with it, formally outlawing institutional membership. Something was said about conflict of interest.

Institutions never really wanted to become members. They were and are in the business of managing money. Most institutions had other reasons too for not wanting to become, however remotely, members of the NYSE. As members, they would be forced to remit all commission savings to their customers. And that would mean the end of all those things that soft dollars bought. Even without the dancing girls, it was a hell of a lot— a lot of research and expert opinion backing up how right you were to make what in retrospect turned out to be a lousy investment judgment. But fixed commissions had by now become a matter of public awareness. Lawsuits were being filed against the institutions for "wasting" customers' money. They had to do something, if only to protect their own fiduciary images.

Given the choice between negotiable commissions and fixed commissions (with soft-dollar perks), most institutions would probably have opted for the preservation of the status quo. But by the 1970s there was no doubt which way the wind was blowing. The institutions had to jump on the negotiating bandwagon and even become wagonmasters.

More cracks in the walls of the Club.

The attack against the SEC was growing, too. On October 22, 1970, the agency permitted the Exchange to increase commission rates for individuals but mandated that all trades over $100,000 in value were no longer subject to fixed commission charges and that such charges could be negotiated.

The Street had no quarrel with the first part (increased charges for individuals), but it went to war over the second part. Negotiate indeed! That was the road to poverty and the end of Wall Street, securities markets, and the American way of life. The fight was led by Bernard Lasker, chairman of the Board of Governors of the NYSE, head of Lasker Stone & Stern (a floor-trader member), and incidentally one of President Nixon's best friends on Wall Street. Somehow SEC Chairman Hamer Budge was made to see how unreasonable his organization had been. The SEC kept the individual increases but raised to $500,000 the level at which negotiations on commission charges could begin.

The SEC's erratic behavior was untenable, and it knew it. It was just a matter of time. Institutions now accounted for the principal share of Wall Street's revenues; fixed commissions simply couldn't be justified when single transactions amounting to millions of dollars were becoming daily occurrences. Thus, in April 1972, the SEC finally demanded that negotiating for commissions begin at the $300,000 level, and the Club capitulated. And after May 1, 1975, commissions on all trades were to be subject to negotiation.

As fixed commissions went, so went the potency of the Club.

Institutions are now forced to look for the best price for the best ability to execute transactions. To know which brokerage firm will get the *very* best price for a particular stock, whether buying or selling, can never be a certainty. As long as institutions deal with acknowledged leaders in the field, some degree of play will exist in the allocation of commission dollars. It may be harder at times to find a buyer for a million shares of AT&T than it is to find a buyer for the same number of shares of Polaroid. And the brokerage firm should be paid extra for its effort. Sometimes it may not be harder and someone will have to keep watch or some form of the soft-dollar bazaar will continue. Today negotiated commissions are saving the customers of institutional investors millions of dollars. Unfortunately, part of that tab is being picked up in the higher rates now charged to the individual investor. That's why you're the most popular kid on the block.

Historians will probably view the era of fixed commissions as a travesty of American justice for the personal profit of a few Club members. It's too bad that history can't also record that the fight against price gouging was led by the government agencies that are sworn to protect the interest of the public. Rather, history will show that two men, radically different from each other, caused right to beat might.

One was Abe Pomerantz, whose attack on the mutual funds compelled the funds to challenge fixed rates. The other was Don Weeden, who by openly defying all the rules of the Club he could have belonged to, forced the Club to change. Ironically, those changes eventually forced him out of the business. They may also force the Club to close its doors.

Don Weeden saw no need for his firm, Weeden & Co., to become a member of the New York Stock Exchange. He tried to run a brokerage firm the way he wanted to. The way he wanted to scared the hell out of the Club.

Weeden & Co. was the most visible member of what came to be known as the Third Market. In an age of institutional business, with trades of large blocks of stocks (often hundreds of thousands of shares in a single order), the mechanics of the

NYSE simply couldn't handle the demand. You can't just call
Merrill Lynch, order a million AT&T, and expect them to send
the order to the floor of the Exchange. You may want to buy
a million AT&T, but the likelihood of your finding someone
with a million to sell waiting for you on the Exchange floor
defies probability.

The Club's answer was the block trading firm. Many members of the NYSE began to develop the relationships and expertise to bring together buyers and sellers of large blocks. Sometimes buyers and sellers could be matched quickly; sometimes
not. When buyers and sellers were finally brought together,
the trade would be executed at the current price on the floor
of the NYSE. In reality, the order would never get to the floor.
But it would show on the tape, and fixed commissions would
be charged to both buyer and seller.

However, the Third Market developed an alternative way
of doing business. It had occurred to Weeden, and to the heads
of a dozen or so similar firms, that they might be able to do
a profitable business and still save money for institutions. Not
being members of the Club, they were not bound by Club
rules; they would deal directly with the institutions. When a
Prudential or a Chase had a block of stock to sell, Weeden
would offer to buy it with its own money. If AT&T were selling
at 60, they might offer to buy 100,000 shares at a net price
of $5,975,000. (That was a better price than the institution
could get if a NYSE member found a buyer at $60 a share
and then subtracted his fixed commission.) Weeden & Co.
would then try to find a buyer for the 100,000 shares and reverse the process.

This company wasn't offering research or fancy lunches. It
was offering customers a chance to save some money while
it made some. But the effect was obvious; however one looked
at it, Weeden Co. was reducing commission charges. Thus it
was attacking one of the most sacred precepts of Wall Street.
The Club was outraged, yet its response was as archaic as its
structure.

The Club did two things. First, it let the banks know that

it would not look favorably on bank trust managers who had anything to do with the Third Market. Members of the NYSE collectively keep enormous amounts in checking accounts (non-interest-earning deposits) with commercial banks. The Club threatened each major bank with the withdrawal of those accounts. Moreover, Club members borrow hundreds of millions of dollars from banks that they reloan to customers as margin loans for securities. That makes brokers very good banking clients. The banks fell into line.

Second, the Club invoked rule 394 (now rule 390), which prohibited members from executing any transaction off the floor of the NYSE. This meant effectively that no member of the Exchange could do business with Weeden Co. or with any member of the Third Market.

Enough was enough! Don Weeden had wanted to run a business in a quiet, legal way. True, the Third Market as a whole had taken away Club business, but the amount involved was less than 10 percent. Weeden decided to fight. He came out of the industry closet and waged war against the established vested interests that the Club had so long preserved.

The Club didn't know whom it was dealing with. Don Weeden cared more about principle than he did about money. He attacked the Exchange's system of fixed rates in speeches, articles, conferences, even on television. He held up the Club's dirty laundry in public and he took it to Washington. Way back in 1965 an SEC study showed that in a sample of 123 trades, 85 percent would have given the customer better prices in the Third Market than they could have received on the Exchange. Weeden started people talking. With lawyers like Abe Pomerantz listening, waiting to ask why institutions, with a fiduciary responsibility to their customers, would knowingly pay higher rather than lower prices, the fixed commission structure was in more trouble.

In 1972 a congressional Subcommittee on Commerce and Finance issued a report that was a triumph for Weeden. The report said that "rule 394 results in an artificial inflation of the amount of commissions charged by member firms and a corresponding increase in the costs of transactions to customers. To the extent that rule 394 also acts to inhibit member firms from seeking best execution off the floor, customers suffer additional economic losses."

Weeden the businessman probably thought the Exchange would give up rule 394 before it gave up fixed commissions. But 394 was the Club's life. It changed it only in minor ways (which is why it is now rule 390). The rule still proscribes members' dealing away from the Exchange. Instead the Club gave up fixed rates.

Weeden thought that his efforts would lead to the member firms being allowed to deal with him. Ironically, his efforts did much to allow all firms to offer the one service that was his firm's raison d'être: low prices. Weeden & Co. became superfluous. It disappeared.

Rule 390 remains a big question mark. It has enormous implications for the individual investor. And it will probably be eliminated soon, so watch out!

If NYSE member firms are allowed to transact business "off the floor," it means that your order to buy 100 shares of anything will no longer be sent to the Exchange where, if you watch carefully, you can see your order cross the tape and read the price of transaction. Without rule 390 Merrill, Blyth, and the other biggies (soon they'll probably be the only ones left) can take all of a day's orders and match them up. For example, on any given day Merrill Lynch probably receives thousands of small orders to buy or sell AT&T. Aggregated, this might mean orders to both buy and sell a million shares. It would be easier and cheaper for Merrill simply to cross those orders on its own books, to debit and credit each customer's account. But at what price to you, the customer? At whatever price they set! You won't have the convenience of the NYSE for easy reference and guide to what you should have paid or been paid. Essentially, all markets will function as the over-the-counter market functions today. The opportunities for cost savings, to you and the firm, will be great. So will be the opportunities for cheating. And that only goes one way. The only way you'll have to keep your broker honest is to let him know that, at least every now and again, you check prices with other firms. Otherwise, you're O.K. if he's O.K. But maybe he's not.

In any event, fixed commission rates are now a thing of the past, and the Club is gasping. Take away 390, and the Club is dead.

GOING FOR BROKE

I have a friend who is a philosopher. She understands Heidegger and Kierkegaard and even existentialism. She teaches all of them to people who don't understand them.

She also has a sizable securities portfolio. Only it's not as sizable as it used to be. She's very philosophical about it. She doesn't know much about the workings of securities markets. Professionals are handling her money, and professionals are losing her money. Therefore no one can figure out the market. Quod erat demonstrandum. Or so she thinks.

My friend understands that when the stock market goes up, you make money, and that when it goes down, you lose money. The time to be in the market is when it's going up. The time to be out is when it's not. But if you leave the market when it begins to go down, what are brokers supposed to do? Study philosophy?

What my friend doesn't understand is the psychology of brokers. They are human and find it hard to be wrong. And since they usually think the market is going up, they're wrong a lot. My friend is a good thinker. If she ever thought about the market, I'd bet she would know when to be in and when to be out. I'd bet she would have a far better track record than her broker, not on picking stocks—she can leave that to him—but on when to be in and when to be out. Her brains are better than his.

I don't want to be simplistic, but when the market goes up, it means that most companies are showing increases in the price of their stock. The odds of picking those stocks are in your favor. When the market goes down, so do your odds. Sure, some stock prices buck the trend, but you've got to be a very good picker. It's like swimming in a lightning storm: you aren't sure to get killed, but common sense says it's a good idea to get out of the water.

Companies are worth what they will earn in the future, just as a dress is worth the pleasure you'll get from wearing it, not while it's on the rack, but next week, next month, or next year—in the future. If you think you'll enjoy wearing it, it's worth more to you than if you think you won't.

Stock prices increase when the stock-buying public believes that companies will do well in the future, that people will buy a company's products and cause the company's profits to increase.

Today every schoolchild knows the words inflation and recession. Every other news broadcast tells us that prices are rising faster than income and that people are becoming poorer. When you have less money, you buy fewer products. It seems to follow that the companies that make those products will thus sell less—and consequently earn less.

If on the average all companies earn less, we have a recession. Companies are not worth more when they are selling less. And stock prices don't increase when companies are earning less.

In a period of high inflation and threatening recession, what can one expect from the stock market? The odds don't look good. Inflation causes all prices to increase, even the price of money. Today one can lend money to the United States government and earn 10 percent a year. You can earn even more by lending to General Motors and more yet by lending to some lesser-known but still very solid companies.

If you can make 10 percent or 10½ percent on your money without risk, by how much does your stock portfolio have to increase in value in order to justify your holding it? At this writing the Dow Jones Average is in the 850 range. To justify your owning stocks it has to increase by more than the 10 percent you can get on bonds—I think a lot more. Ten percent alone means that the market would go to 935; 20 percent would put it over 1,000.

Maybe that will happen. But with inflation, recession, rising oil prices, a falling dollar (foreigners won't want to buy the products of American companies because they are too expensive), and a guaranteed 10 percent return on your money waiting for you on any street corner, why would anyone want to be in the market? Because brokers don't read philosophy. Because they think *la vie en rose.* Because if you don't buy, they don't eat.

So brokers always think that the market is about to go up. Or they hope so, and they transmit that hope to you. And if they don't think that everything will go up, they always have some interesting situation that they think will.

I like the stock market. I like being in it. But only when the odds are in my favor. They were in my favor in 1971 and again in 1974. After 1976 the odds turned, and so did anyone who read the newspapers. The newspapers, not the brokers, told us the odds were in our favor again in March 1978.

That's when President Carter put his foot down. Enough inflation; wage and price guidelines were in. Enough erosion of the dollar; $30 billion would be spent to bolster its position on international markets. Carter took a stand, and America and the rest of the world liked it. Things looked good for the American economy. The stock market went up.

Then came October 1978. It was apparent that nothing was happening. It didn't show so much on the business pages, but it was written across the front pages of all the newspapers in the country. The public was losing confidence. Carter couldn't do a thing about George Meany or inflation, and he couldn't do much for the dollar. The odds had changed again. Out!

I'm not always so smart. But I am always a coward. I'm afraid to lose money. I figure it this way: If I'm wrong (and the market goes up), I will still make 10 percent on my money. Other

people may make more, but I can always change my mind
and return to the market if conditions change. If I'm right, I
will also make 10 percent on my money, and I can wait until
the next 1974 comes along. How much will you have left if I
was right and your broker was wrong? In this business the
coward's allegiance to the stock market dies many times; the
brave man's money often just dies.

My philosopher friend is wrong; there is a logic to the stock
market. There is also a logic to stockbrokerage. It's just that
the two are not always the same. And if you're in there playing
the game, you have to be able to discern the difference. Wall
Street is betting that you won't be able to do it.

Most people won't. They won't take the time. Perhaps sub-
consciously people like to lose money; maybe they like to be
disappointed. So the Club may die, but the Street won't. The
environmental changes that the Exchange closed its eyes to
were not missed by the smarter members of the Wall Street
community. Some of the less smart died; some of the more
forward-thinking sold out or merged. In the early 1960s there
were 681 firms that were members of the Exchange. By 1975
there were 505. The number is well below 500 today, and
the shakeout hasn't ended yet.

From Wall Street's point of view, the new game is the retail
customer and the new "service" is all the products you can
be persuaded to buy. You may think of yourself as an investor.
But the new Wall Street sees in you a customer for stocks,
bonds, new issues (underwriting), commodities, options, tax
shelters, mutual funds, and municipals. And that's only the
beginning. Merrill Lynch is prepared to sell you a new house
or to lend you money. Soon you'll be able to transfer funds
directly from your margin account to settle your Visa or Master
Charge statements. The brokerage industry of the near future
will try to take care of every aspect of your financial life and
other areas as well. To do this, firms will need capital—big
capital—and a new wave of consolidations and mergers may
be expected. The single office broker may well be as anachro-
nistic as the ma and pa grocery store, and a new group of

giant brokers may soon rival banks, both in size and in business.

Just as you are the customer of the future, the customer's man—the retail stockbroker—is the Wall Streeter of the future. And he's being solicited today as though he were going out of style.

Wall Street firms have always raided one another, luring away each other's top researchers, corporate finance men, and institutional salespeople with higher salaries, bigger offices, higher percentages of commission payouts. The tide has turned. All eyes now focus on the big retail producer. Anyone on the Street who produces even as much as $100,000 in gross commissions for a firm is getting calls from other firms. If his own firm is giving him 25 percent of the gross, another will make it 30 percent. When Merrill Lynch acquired White Weld & Co. in 1978, the plum was the more than 450 White Weld retail salespeople, who generated an average of $120,000 a year each in commissions, an amount substantially above the industry average of $66,000 and somewhat better than the $100,000 a year that Merrill Lynch's 7,600 salespeople averaged.

No sooner was the merger announced than most of those 450 superstars began receiving calls offering to better any deal that Merrill Lynch made. Donald Regan, chairman of Merrill Lynch and one of the most innovative men on the Street, finally had to give a 10 percent bonus to the White Weld people for the first three months and another 5 percent for the next three. Nevertheless the casualty list was high. According to *Fortune* magazine, individual salespeople and even entire office staffs were vanishing only to resurface intact at one of the other twenty or so large firms. Blyth Eastman Dillon picked up the manager and seven of the eight White Weld salespeople in Omaha; they got the manager of the New Haven office too, along with fifteen of the twenty salespeople there. A. G. Becker got eight of the fourteen in Minneapolis, and a dozen crossed a London street to Paine Webber.

Merrill Lynch thought the White Weld deal included 450 brokers. By last count they ended up with less than half that number. What Merrill Lynch had paid for, others ended up getting for free. Blyth Eastman Dillon was the biggest winner, adding at least sixty former White Weldians to their nationwide network. Not that Merrill Lynch hasn't done or wouldn't do the same thing. But this mauling of Merrill Lynch was spectacular. Merrill Lynch had offered those guys bonuses to stay. Imagine what the other firms must have offered them to leave! And all for *you*.

That's the point here: all those payouts, all those bonuses, all the double-dealing that once went into stealing people who could increase institutional business, all that effort is now directed at procuring the people who can procure you. The day of the retail customer has indeed come. In wartime it was Uncle Sam who wanted you; now it's Uncle Wally. And he has a lot of different things to sell, enough of a variety that he'll find something to turn you on and—if you're not smart— to turn your pockets out.

In 1978 and 1979 the big flyers were the gambling stocks. Resorts International, Caesars World, and Bally Manufacturing headed a long list. While General Motors trades at seven times earnings and AT&T at eight times earnings, some of these gambling companies' shares are selling for up to one hundred times current earnings. The last time stocks sold that high they heralded the crash of 1973. I draw no parallels, except to note that those prices for gambling indicate that people think the companies are going to do fabulously well—more than ten times better in relative earnings appreciation than GM. It could be!

What I'd like to know is what the brokers are telling their clients who hold those stocks. And their clients who want to buy them now. How many brokers were caught with their pants and clients down when Resorts International fell from 220 to 80? Did those brokers think Resorts was worth $220 based on what they believed the company's future earning power to be? Did they think that gambling would be the new wonder drug of the 1980s? That Atlantic City would pack in a whole new crowd without diminishing the take in Las Vegas

and Reno? That every state in the Union would join in the
fun and that casinos would replace nursing homes? Did anyone
bother to realize that even though the profits posted by Resorts
International's Atlantic City operation exceeded all expectations, they did so while Resorts was the only casino legally
operating on the east coast? When other casinos joined the
Atlantic City melee, were we to believe that each would draw
upon an ever-increasing gambling population rather than di-
vide a finite one? If they did, perhaps they can be excused.
When the market took the stock from 220 to 80, it apparently
didn't agree.

It's my bet that the recommending brokers were playing
the "bigger fool" theory. That theory is one of Wall Street's
oldest and most often used justifications for buying stocks at
any price; it holds that you might be a fool to pay more for a
company than it seems to be worth, but you don't need to
worry because there will always be a bigger fool willing to
pay you more. That's how lots of brokers make a lot of money.
The only problem, as any ten-year-old can figure out, is that
somewhere in this finite universe there exists the biggest fool.
Sometimes it's you.

This year's gambling craze brings back memories of the nursing home insanity that caught the imagination (or fantasy) of
the public not so many years ago. Remember Four Seasons
Nursing Homes? It was crooked and went bust. I have to assume
that the gambling companies are honest, so there are no com-
parisons to be made there. But there are similarities in the
price actions of the stocks. In each case market fever took
these companies to heights that could never be justified by
earnings.

In the late 1960s the government began to provide large
sums of money for nursing home and postoperative care. Four
Seasons, a construction company, saw the future and decided
to be a part of it. It began building nursing homes as fast as
it could get the bricks.

Walston & Co. was an early financer of the company. (That
was not one of its better decisions, but it wouldn't know that

for a while.) Walston paid about 50 cents a share for its initial investment. A few years later it brought the company public at $11 a share.

Four Seasons was making money even though its own projections of the number of beds needed for the company to break even weren't being met. The stock went to $50 six months after it first hit the market. Walston did a secondary offering. This time 50 percent of the money raised went to the Walston partners who were selling their own shares; the rest went to Four Seasons. The stock went to $100. Four Seasons formed another company to raise mortgage money to finance the parent. The spin-off went public and reached about $50 a share while the parent went to $150, then to $200.

Four Seasons decided to go into franchising. Higher and higher projections of future earnings came from management and then from the Wall Street security analysts who believed what management told them.

While the company reported actual earnings of $1.63, the stock approached $300—nearly two hundred times actual earnings! That was like paying $9 for an ice cream cone; it doesn't, didn't, and couldn't make sense—not then, not ever. But the brokers had latched on to something that fired the imagination of the public, and they weren't about to let go.

Smart people took their profits and fled. But tens of thousands of individuals—and, surprisingly, institutions—did not. They didn't want to be left out of the action. They just kept on buying, bidding the price higher and higher. The price of air was going up.

It's anticlimactic to report that it would have taken billions of dollars for Four Seasons to build enough homes to have any of its fantastic projections approach reality—and that there was no way that the company could raise those billions. It's equally anticlimactic to report that the annual report that showed the $1.63 profit had a back section: dark blue paper filled with black figures that no normal eyes could read. These were the footnotes, and they reported that all the while the company was in fact losing money. Yet the stock price kept going up anyway! No one was going to be bothered with the facts—or detoured by them.

Four Seasons got as high as $350 a share before it floated to $1. From 11 to 350 to 1 over a span of two years. That's market fever, exhilarating—and terminal.

Since most brokers spend most of their time at their desks, pressing stock quotation machine buttons for customers on the phone and checking prices six times a day, they have little time to think about the actual worth of companies. They sound smart because they often have memos from the research department that they can quote to you. And when they don't have memos, those little machines, at the press of another set of buttons, will give you highs, lows, dividends, earnings—all sorts of information. If you're on the phone, you can't see your friendly broker pressing buttons. It sounds as though he has all that information at the top of his head. Impressive as hell. The guy must be awfully smart! Lucky he's your broker.

Brokers as a group don't study companies themselves. Some do; some used to be security analysts and know how to evaluate the information sent to them. Some even do further work on their own. But from my experience, most do not.

I called a broker after the nuclear accident in Pennsylvania. My parents own a bundle of long-term bonds of several utilities around the country. I wanted to know whether any of those utilities were involved with nuclear power and what the possible ramifications might be. These were perfectly reasonable questions, I thought.

It didn't take him a second to answer. "Whatta ya worried about? All those bonds are rated A or AA." I began to protest but then realized it was no use. Sure, those bonds were rated A or AA—before the accident! I asked instead for the name of the guy who researches utilities.

Most brokers at the major New York Stock Exchange firms get their information from two sources, the firm's research department and the firm's corporate finance (underwriting) department. When a major firm commits itself to underwrite or to be part of a syndicate to sell a new issue of securities, it is the job of the broker to see that those securities get placed. He doesn't have to offer his own customers issues he thinks are crap. But discernment is not usually a broker's highest quality. New issues sold to the public net of commission usually mean a somewhat higher take for the broker, particularly if they prove in any way difficult to place.

How often I've received those calls! "I've got this new issue, it's speculative but it really looks good." "This big prestigious firm is putting its name behind the issue." It looks like "a growing industry," it's an "interesting situation," it's "the wave of the future." Oh, they know the buzz words. But no difference; somewhere in there the broker said *speculative*, the key word for his conscience. Like the lover who never said out loud, "I love you," having put that word in, however softly or quickly, means there's no need to mention it again. He murmured it, and whether you know it or not, so far as he's concerned, you're now on your own.

Corporate underwriting can be a very lucrative profit center for a major firm. Bringing a new company public can mean large fees; it can also mean large profits on the stock the firm originally took for itself as a part of its fee, particularly if the company goes public at a higher price.

The underwriting business hasn't been too good in the last few years. The General Motors and Exxons have all been taken. When they issue new securities, their underwriters handle it. When they don't, corporate finance departments have to look for the new companies that might be the year's hit. Those departments tend to do what all the other firms do. And recently it's been gambling. The seemingly good gambling companies chose their underwriters and raised their money. But what about the underwriters who missed out? Many went looking for, trying to discover, new companies that were related to, or could be construed as being related to, gambling. When they found them, they brought them public. (I'm not talking about the "bucket shops," the underwriters who fall in the "now you see them, now you don't" category.) Big member firms of the NYSE want to increase their underwriting business to the limit. Sometimes they try too hard, and then they give us less than their best judgment.

We only have to recall the 1960s, when "hot issues" were the rage and everyone wanted to get at least a few shares of the latest computer- or technology-related company at the offering price. Those were the days when a company would go public at 10 A.M. at $8 a share and be selling for $30 before the market closed. Institutions would gobble up those new issues (given as yet another form of payment for commission dollars), and maybe, if you were a good retail account, your broker might have pleaded for 10 shares for you.

Most of the high-flying companies of that go-go era proved to be shooting stars, and most often we were lucky to have been passed over. Careful tabulation would probably show that the less glamorous new issues of the decade, the ones we could have had our fill of since no one else really cared about them, proved to be the more solid investments.

That supposition notwithstanding, certain dangers lurk for the individual investor in the new issue market.

When a company is being brought to the market for the first time by a respected brokerage firm, or when a new class of securities is being offered, indications of interest in participating in that new issue are first sought from the major financial institutions. That may not seem fair, but that's how it ought to be. An interested institution might take 10 percent of an issue, and that makes the job of selling it much easier. Another issue may be too small for a large bank or mutual fund to care about. That doesn't mean it's a bad investment. And that's one of the reasons why retail firms like Merrill Lynch have achieved their preeminent position in securities underwriting: with thousands of salespeople and more than a million customers, such a firm can almost guarantee that a new issue will be placed successfully with the public.

Sometimes, however, firms find that they have underwritten securities that, for whatever reason, the institutions just won't take. These may be companies that will do very well in the future, but for the present something about them has turned the big buyers off. That's when your phone will ring and your broker will give you a spiel about this or that new issue. Don't hang up, but do wonder why he's being so kind to you, particularly if he tells you that you can have all you want. Certainly the institutions don't know everything. One only has to look at the banks' records in managing trust or pension accounts. Or at the recent performance of mutual funds. A skeptical view toward gift horses never hurts.

Not long ago I was quietly minding my own business, happily pushing the buttons on a Quotron machine in the New York office of a major New York Stock Exchange firm. Suddenly a voice came over the retail sales office intercom. It announced that the time was now 3:30 P.M., half an hour until the markets would close at 4 P.M. A new issue of preferred stock had come out that day, the firm had a large chunk of it to dispose of, and it wasn't moving very well.

Nothing wrong here, I thought; just a little pep talk to get the sales force moving. Then the voice added that the lottery was on! On Wall Street? A major firm? A lottery? Well, perhaps it was just a little extra commission for the guy who placed the most shares in the next half hour.

I went on pushing buttons, as if that would make any of my own stocks move faster.

At 4 P.M. on the dot a man called for quiet. It was time to announce the winner. Everyone stood on their chairs or moved up close. Lots of applause, as though someone were retiring and was about to get a gold watch. And the winner is. . . . A young man stepped forward. More applause. Mr. Young Man had sold 6,000 shares in thirty minutes. Oohs and ahs. More applause. Someone shouted that he had probably dumped them on his mother. Some boos. Then, as on those television quiz shows, the MC took a wad of bills from his pocket. Ten, twenty, thirty—some secretaries took the cue and started counting along—forty, fifty, sixty. Soon the entire office had joined in the chant, 200 . . . 400 . . . 500 . . . 550, 560, 570, 580, 590, 600. A $600 cash bonus for selling 6,000 shares! Good thing they didn't give this guy a whole hour.

My questions are simple ones. Granted, most of us are moti-
vated by reward, cash or otherwise; but who were the people
that this guy and all the other salespeople were calling? Did
he believe that they ought to buy that stock? Was it a good
investment for his clients (who must have some degree of confidence in his judgment)? Or was he thinking of the extra money
for that special effort?

I hope the stock goes up so that the buyers' investment decision proves right. But I have a gnawing feeling that if the
stock does go up, the decision will have been right, but for
the wrong reasons. This is just another argument for getting
to know your broker. And for letting him know what you know.
Maybe then, when he does call, it will be because he's really
proud of what he's selling.

The firm's research department is the broker's second major
source of information for dissemination to customers. If you
rely on your broker for suggestions, it's a good idea to have
a broker at a firm with a proven research department. We've
heard about the superstars, the analysts with the $100,000-plus
salaries. Remember, they earn those salaries by recommending
the companies that you, and the institutions, buy. If they are
wrong too often, they might get fired. Lots do. A lot of others
hedge a lot, building up and then living on their reputations.
They may strike gold every now and again, but often their
records stink. And that's why so many investors lose money.

Good or bad, right or wrong, every major firm comes out
with a list of recommended stocks. And from that list each
broker culls his own recommendations. The list, of course,
changes over time. The categories are "buy," "sell," and "hold."
"Buy" means that the analyst has convinced the research director or the sales committee or some person or group that the
stock in question is undervalued and will increase in price.
"Sell" means get out quick. "Hold" is somewhat abstruse: it
may mean that the stock has not moved, we expected it to
and maybe it still will; that the stock has gone down, but we
pray it will go up; that the stock has gone up and we think
it will rise a few more points; or, too bad, I made a mistake,

the company's a bomb, but I don't want to admit it—maybe I can get away with it for a while and change to sell later. Funny, Wall Street, by count, puts out many more buy recommendations than sell ones. Back again to wishful thinking.

If your broker does a modicum of work other than telephoning, he knows the track record of each analyst and can make intelligent recommendations. (You'll still have to decide for yourself whether it's time to be buying at all.) But don't count on that extra work. It's not often necessary since most people seem to have two predispositions: (1) loyalty to stockbrokers, which comes from (2) believing that they (the investors) actually make their own decisions and use their brokers only for purposes of substantiating information. Would that this were true. Brokers have much more influence on most investors than the investor is ever willing to allow. I would never diagnose my own medical condition; yet it's incredible how many doctors, lawyers, and Indians think they are experts in the market. They are the type that brokers can nudge so easily with their latest report from the research department.

Since it's your money, you might want to take a look at some of the reports the research guys write. You might even want to see what they wrote in the past. Some research analysts actually have terrific records, and you might want to stick with them rather than with their firms' "recommended" list.

It doesn't take much checking to find out, for example, that David Londoner of Wertheim & Co. is pretty much regarded as the world expert on Disney. Just for the fun of it, I asked David to give me all of the Disney recommendations, buy and sell, that he printed over the last fourteen years. I did a quick calculation which did not include any money that you would have earned at interest during the periods between sell recommendations and "time to buy again" reports. My figures showed that a $10,000 investment in 1965, followed by strict adherence to David's buys and sells, including his mistakes (and he made a few), would be worth $190,000 today. Even with inflation, that's not bad.

But Londoner is willing to say that he's made a mistake and

advise you to cut your losses. A good security analyst knows there will be another day. There are lots of good analysts and brokers out there, just as good as Londoner, and they have the records to prove it. It may be worth your while to look around.

Sometimes brokers go with the craze. That craze could be gambling, or it could be the latest "hot" analyst. There's nothing particularly wrong with that, just so long as you remember that anyone can make a mistake and that the best way for you to minimize yours is by using the stop loss order.

Look, if a broker recommends and you buy and the stock goes down, don't expect the broker to tell you to sell. He can't: it forces him to admit he's a dope. He won't. Therefore, set your own limits—10 percent, 15 percent, 20 percent at most. If the value of your purchase declines by that amount, sell! There will always be another day—unless you insist that you can't be wrong. Then you will sit with your mistakes, waiting for them to at least get back to what you paid for them. Meanwhile, you're losing out on something really good, and at the very least the interest on your money. You don't have to be right all the time to make money in the market. But if you *believe* that you have to be right, holding on to a mistake can wipe you out.

In case you didn't know it, contrary to all popular myth, there is no such thing as a stock market "tip." There is only information. Sometimes you might get it ahead of the crowd because you have a good broker or a good researcher. Sometimes you can figure it out before they do—like Atlantic City. But the people who bought Resorts International early didn't do it on a tip. They did it because they were willing to take the odds that (1) Atlantic City would be allowed to legalize gambling and (2) Resorts would be granted a license. Those people weren't privy to inside information. For months the papers were filled with the debate over the New Jersey referendum and its implications for various companies. The early people were brave. Consciously or not, they measured the possible risk against the possible reward. No inside info, no secret telephone calls, no special privilege. Just a weighing of alternatives. Sure, every now and again someone finds out about a merger or about a new contract before the press release. But this doesn't happen as often as it used to—or as reliably.

These days a "tip" is more apt to be a research analyst's new findings about a company. The word is bound to get out in advance of the printed report. But if your broker passes on that kind of information to you, try to make sure that he knows what he's talking about. Or wait another day or two until he does (stock prices don't move so quickly that single days are urgent). Otherwise, you might find that your broker is passing on something he heard at lunch and may never hear about again. Brokers are notorious for picking up tidbits from rival firms' research departments (the "grass is always greener" syndrome). Try to exercise a little caution, particularly when the broker thinks it's a good stock for you but he doesn't have room for it in his own portfolio.

Just as a major problem with brokers is a singular inability to suggest that a stock you bought on their recommendation should be sold at a loss, the problem with taking tips is that the tipster usually forgets who it was he tipped. (Of course, we assume that no one would be foolish enough to take a "tip" from someone obviously unqualified to give one.)

In my day I've taken some tips. But they came from Wall Street friends, people in the business whose investment judgment I trust. In these cases a "tip" has usually been of the sort where a friend just happens to mention that some analyst, well-respected and known to be right more often than wrong, has just strongly recommended that XYZ Airline be bought. My friend and I are most probably having a once-in-three-months drink. After the information has been passed on to me, he'll go about his business and I about mine. If we're both lucky, the stock will go up. Then, later, something may change. The airline analyst—my friend's friend, remember, not mine—revises his outlook: time to sell the stock. My friend gets the news quickly. But does he happen to recall that one day, over a second martini, he got me involved, too? It would be nice

to think so, but the odds are he doesn't. After that initial pass-
along, you're on your own.

This happened to me a few years ago. Bally Manufacturing,
makers of pinball machines, one-armed bandits, and all the
other toys that go into gambling casinos, certainly ranks as
one of the hot stocks of 1978, 1979, and maybe 1980. In 1972
it was hot too.

One day I had a luncheon appointment with a leading Wall
Street analyst. When I arrived at 12:15 P.M., his 10 A.M. meeting
was still going on (it had something to do with merging two
companies and a $50,000 bonus if he pulled it off). He inter-
rupted the meeting and came out pressed and apologetic.
Couldn't have lunch, had to continue, too much at stake, knew
I'd understand, do you have any extra money around? Buy
Bally.

What the hell did I want with more shoes? (Quick glance
down to see if mine were unpolished or run down at the heels.)
"Not shoes, jerk—gambling!"

"Why?" I had to talk fast, knowing he had to get back to
his bonus. Yet I had a firm grip on his tie.

"Don't ask dumb questions," he replied. "No time to explain.
Do you think I'd pass on garbage?"

So I took $3,300 and bought 100 shares. I trusted him, but
not for more than the vacation money I had sitting in a savings
bank. And not even for very much of that. When I phoned
in my order, I told my broker to sell it if it fell to 30. I didn't
know what I was doing, other than that I was gambling on
gambling. And since I never walk into a casino with more
than $100 in my pocket, I figured that play in a casino stock
was worth only a $300 loss.

Sure enough, Bally started moving up, to 38 within a week.
I called my broker. "Sell if it falls to 35." It kept going up,
to 45. "Sell at 42," I ordered. As the stock went up, I kept
ordering that it be sold if it went down. It didn't. In six months
the stock went to 66. I'm not greedy; I put in an order to
sell at 63. This time I got hit. At 66 the stock turned around
and kept going. But I was out at 63 and not at all unhappy

that my friend couldn't have lunch with me those many months ago.

I didn't hear from him for a while—that's the way it goes in the business—and then he called one Saturday morning. His merger hadn't gone through, but he was doing all right with a lot of other stuff, and by the way don't worry about Bally. I said I wasn't worried. Don't worry, he said, it will come back. Earnings not as good as expected, and the whole market stinks. But don't worry. I asked where Bally was. Sixteen, he said, but don't worry.

Something in the way I said "Gee" must have tipped him off. He asked why I wasn't worried. I told him I had sold it. I didn't want to rub it in, but he demanded to know at what price. I told him. I heard a click at the other end of the line.

I guess we've both been very busy, but it's funny I haven't heard from my friend since.

One sidelight on stockbrokerage: I balance my checkbook, but always consider it an exercise in arithmetic. I check my numbers against those of the bank's computer, and if the totals are different, I do my sums again. In the case of my checkbook I assume that the bank knows what it's doing and will always be right. It always has been. Yet I keep doing the exercise anyway. I have been acculturated: banks don't make mistakes with checking deposits.

Brokerage firms are different. They make lots of mistakes with people's accounts. Most of them are corrected eventually, and perhaps that's too bad. Recently a client opened a trust account for his son with $7,500 in securities. At the end of the month he received a statement of the account's holdings. There it was, right name, right account number, wrong securities. According to the firm, the kid had 1,000 shares of IBM, a mess of AT&T and Exxon, and a few odd lots here and there— about $800,000 worth altogether. It took the firm three months to get it all straightened out, but it finally did. Poor kid.

Back in the late 1960s and early 1970s the firms didn't always get such matters straightened out. Back-office problems got to be so bad that some firms—Goodbody & Co. was the larg-

est—just folded up. It took a few years, but in the end everyone
got their securities back. Some people got even more; they
bought 1,000 shares of Standard of Ohio, for example, and
were credited with 10,000 shares. So they'd put in an order
to sell 10,000 shares and then bank the checks when they arrived. Lots of firms never figured out who got what. Not one
bit like my checking account.

Any stock sold by a broker to the public must be registered
with the SEC. Isn't it logical, then, to assume, if a broker from
a major firm calls to suggest a purchase, that he's offering you
stock that can legally be sold? Don't be so sure.

A few years ago Educational Services Program went public.
The records don't show which underwriter brought the stock
to market, but for a while the stock was a favortie of the late
Walston & Co., in its day one of the Wall Street biggies. A
friend of mine bought a bunch for his clients in the $16–$17
range. After all, one of the firm's analysts thought that it was
a terrific company, that it was going to make loads of money
in the booming business of vocational schooling. (As in those
ads we see on the late late movies: quit your boring job and
become a computer programmer, or learn to drive big trucks
with twenty forward gears.)

However, my friend was the type of broker who did two
things that most brokers are usually too busy to do. First, he
always told his clients that on something speculative, they
ought to sell if the stock declines by 15 percent. That was
his rule, and he stuck to it. He had seen too many stocks, particularly in the 1960s, have great run-ups only to end at zero.
Second, he liked to check out for himself the stocks he was
recommending.

The stock went up; it reached about $40 a share. Then my
friend heard that the president of the company was holding
an explanatory meeting for potential investors at the Waldorf-
Astoria Hotel in New York. So my friend took the afternoon
off. He arrived at the Waldorf to find the president of ESP
surrounded by girls who made Playboy bunnies look as though
they were dressed like Eskimos. He asked a few questions and

soon realized that the guy couldn't run a candy store. My friend
didn't hang around.

Back to the office. Telephone calls to all his customers. Sell!

Six months later my friend got a call from the SEC. Why
had he sold? How come he told his customers to take their
profits and live happily ever after? Why hadn't he reported
what he knew to the SEC?

Report what? How he felt about candy stores?

Eventually the SEC was satisfied and my friend and his
friends got to keep what they made. But the people who held
on to the stock had no luck. It fell to zero. It was a company
whose management didn't know how to do anything right.
In fact it didn't even know how to register the stock—and
Walston & Co. had never bothered to check. That kind of
nonchalance may be one reason why Walston is no longer listed
in telephone directories.

Among modern conveniences and the inventions of the past
decade, none is viewed by most brokerage firms as being more
malevolent than the liquid asset fund. Most Wall Street VIPs
would sooner contract (and recover from) some dread disease
than talk about them; most brokers had better not discuss them
with their customers—and certainly not go on record as having
initiated such a conversation—if they want to keep their jobs.
And most customers haven't a clue as to what they are.

Liquid asset funds are one of the few really good things to
have happened to the ordinary investor in years. They are
the product of what seemed to be exorbitantly high interest
rates in 1973-1974; as a countermeasure, they gave birth to
the now popular six-month savings certificate of deposit—the
kind that this week offers 9.99 percent interest if you don't
touch your money for six months (and heavy penalties for early
withdrawal if you do).

In 1974 interest rates on short-term government securities
passed 9 percent. Everyone was aware of it because Walter
Cronkite and David Brinkley told them about it. Ordinary people began to wonder why their local savings bank was paying
only 5¼ percent on deposits while the government was paying

nearly twice that rate. Maybe it was because savings accounts (up to a certain amount) were guaranteed by the government. After all, who was guaranteeing the bonds and bills of the government itself? A little thought showed that that argument didn't work. Perhaps it was because the savings banks gave toasters or alarm clocks with new deposits. But the idea of a toaster in every room never caught on like television.

Suddenly a new phenomenon emerged: little old ladies who used to lunch at Schrafft's on Wednesdays got wise. They began arranging to meet each other, not at local eateries but on line at the Federal Reserve Bank in their neighborhoods whenever an auction of new Treasury bills was held. They were taking their savings out of those 5¼ percent accounts and putting them into three-month and six-month bills. Not only would they get higher interest rates, but the interest paid on the government bonds, unlike that paid by the banks, was exempt from state and local taxes.

The savings banks panicked. The little old ladies were withdrawing billions from thrift institutions, billions that the banks had been taking in at 5¼ percent and relending, often to the government, at 9 percent. The little old ladies were disintermediating—they were going directly to the ultimate borrower, bypassing the friendly "We're a people bank" intermediary. It just wasn't fair!

Fortunately for the banks, there was a catch. Treasury bills had to be bought in $10,000 denominations, and even in our affluent society not everyone has that kind of loose change sitting around.

That's where mother necessity came in. Some bright mutual funder thought up a fund that bought only short-term instruments of the highest, safest quality—United States government Treasury bills, commercial paper, large commercial bank certificates of deposit (the kind that go for $100,000 or more and pay the highest rates of interest), banker's acceptances, and so forth. These funds could yield at least as much as Treasury bills, even after deducting the fund manager's fee. Since lots of people would be mutually funding, the fund could afford to take subscriptions of less than $10,000. Much less!

The first funds required a minimum deposit of only $500. Thereafter you could add any amount to your account ($7.42, if you felt like it), and you could take your money out at any time without any loss of the daily compounding interest. The funds were an immediate and a great success. But as usual, it was the larger investor who capitalized on them. (Perhaps they read the ads better, or perhaps the unsophisticated public wondered whether the money was guaranteed.)

Here's where the brokerage firms come in. If you have an account with a brokerage firm, there will be times when you have idle money in that account. Say you have just sold 100 AT&T; you have $6,000 in your account and you're not sure what to buy next. You'll make up your mind in a few days. In the meantime the money sits. That's what you think! Brokerage firms aren't dummies. They're taking that $6,000, and $20,000 from another account, and $47.50 from another, and putting that money into short-term paper and the equivalent of the liquid asset funds. And the firms are making bundles. Your idle money (and that of tens of thousands like you) is one of their biggest profit sources. It's money that doesn't cost them anything to lend and the daily interest on that money goes into their pockets. And it's all perfectly legal. Millions of extra dollars a year to pay for firms' fancy television commercials or year-end bonuses.

What can you do about it? Simple: Ask your broker to open an account for you in one of the liquid asset funds. What will it cost you? Nothing! Just instruct your friendly broker to transfer regularly any credit balance in your house account to your liquid trust account. Then you, not the brokerage firm, will get the interest. And when you want to buy something through your broker, the money can be transferred back immediately. But why should it be? You don't have to pay for most things that brokers buy for you for five business days—and five days' interest can add up.

No broker can refuse to perform this function for you. Nor can he charge you for it. And the funds don't charge extra, either—for any number of deposits or withdrawals. All you have to do is ask. Or tell! If you don't, they won't do it for you, because so far there's no law that brokers must always act in your best interest. Like those commission discounts they don't want to talk about. The brokers know damn well that too much talk to too many clients about liquid asset funds won't go over well with top management. And in today's contracting securities business no one wants to mess with the boss.

It must be added that not a few firms have begun to offer their clients interest on their credit balances. But that's only because word of the liquid asset funds is spreading. If you check it out, however, odds are that the brokerage firms are offering less interest (even though it may be more attractively packaged) than you can get through one simple, ongoing instruction to your broker.

Some firms have tried to salvage a piece of the pie in a reprehensible way: one in particular has established its own liquid asset fund and encourages its salespeople to switch clients in other funds to the house fund. So far so good. But the house fund, unlike the public funds, accepts deposits only in $1,000 denominations. If you have $1,999.99 in your brokerage account, $1,000 will go into the interest-earning fund and $999.99 will sit in your account, to be used by the firm for its own "interest."

Of course, if making a few extra bucks isn't your bag, you need only leave things the way they are. You'll be making your brokerage firm very happy. They'll be sure to send you a Christmas card.

4

AMICUS CURIAE

Ever since that time on Sinai when God, through Moses, told the people that, among other things, thou shalt not steal, man and nations have been wondering exactly what God had in mind.

Until the very recent past, it was widely assumed that a separate protocol had been established that exempted the securities industry from God's ordinance. Before 1933, when Congress finally got around to passing the first Securities Act, Wall Street (like the Mafia) meted out its own form of justice. If the Street treated you well, you were judged a capitalist in the best American tradition. If you lost your shirt, it was assumed that you shouldn't have been there in the first place. *Caveat emptor* was the rule of the day, and while selling booze was a crime against the state, stock manipulation, market cornering, selling shares in nonexistent companies, and issuing false or misleading statements about corporations were all considered standard business practices. In a free enterprise system no one bothered to wonder whether there might be anything wrong with a broker's urging a customer to buy shares that the broker himself wanted to unload.

In theory, the establishment of the Securities and Exchange Commission in 1934 was to put an end to all those shenanigans. Henceforth it would be illegal to beggar thy neighbor. Companies were to fully and fairly disclose information to the public;

brokers were to advise clients fairly. No more fooling around.

Some of the more blatant malpractices did indeed stop. But give a clever mind a law, put it to work to find ways around that law, and five will get you ten those ways will be found. Cut a worm in two, and it develops a new second half; take a game away from Wall Street, and it invents a new one.

The establishment of the SEC lulled the public into a false sense of security. Investors rightly believed that they now had a watchdog to protect their interests. What they didn't realize was that so many Wall Street and corporate activities had been established and openly practiced for so long that it would be decades before it would even occur to the SEC that some of them might in fact be illegal.

But the Lord works in strange ways His miracles to perform. Into this world He sent one Abraham L. Pomerantz. It was probably meant as some perverse inside joke between God and the Angels of the Board, perhaps to show that the David who whipped the Philistines into shape was not a one-time happenstance. Corporate hubris had reached its pinnacle in the 1920s; so God sent a messenger to turn the corporate and securities world on its collective ear.

Abraham Pomerantz was born in Brooklyn and grew up to become an American socialist. To him making a lot of money and caring about the plight of the not so rich were not mutually exclusive. He went to law school in the days before you had to go to college first, and he got his degree in 1924. He took his first job working for another lawyer but figured $4 a week wasn't much to give up. He struck out on his own. With three other lawyers and a stenographer (all in one room), he opened up shop and waited for clients. When no client was around, the group played knock-rummy. They played a lot of knock-rummy. The occasional client paid the bills, but Pomerantz wasn't exactly a success. By 1932 he had a wife, two children, and no exciting prospects.

Then God gave Abraham a sign. It appeared in the guise of Celia Gallin, the widow of his high school gym teacher. It seems her husband had left her 20 shares of stock in the National City Bank of New York. Before the crash of 1929 the

stock had sold for as much as $585 a share. In those days $11,700
wasn't bad money. You could buy a whole house for that
amount and still have some left over. But after the crash the
stock fell to $17 a share, and the widow's fortune dwindled
to $340. She wondered if there might be someone to sue. Pom-
erantz said there was no law against losing money, and the
lady went home.

Had the widow not presented her case, our hero might not
have paid much attention to an investigation of stock market
practices begun soon afterward by the Senate Banking Committee. One witness called by Ferdinand Pecora, the committee counsel, was the chairman of National City Bank, Charles
E. Mitchell. While being questioned, Mitchell let it drop that
the bank engaged in the rather curious practice of setting aside
a large percentage of its profits to be paid as incentive bonuses
to the chairman and other principal officers. This neat arrangement had netted Mitchell $608,868 over and above his salary,
and that was just for the first six months of 1929. Some incentive! The sound of the angel's horn was becoming distinctly
audible.

The rage of the socialist found outlet in the imagination of
the lawyer. Pomerantz phoned his once-prospective client. He
explained that he still couldn't turn her $17 shares back into
$585 shares, but he said that if she would agree to sue, there
was some chance that Mitchell and his friends could be forced
to return their bonus money. At best her shares would be worth
only a few cents more, since any judgment would have to be
apportioned among all stockholders. But it was an opportunity
for some retribution. And she had nothing to lose; Pomerantz
would charge no fee if he lost. He won.

With his team of lawyers assembled, Pomerantz attacked
the establishment. He charged that the National City Bank
was wasting corporate assets. How God and His company must
have chuckled: $1,800,000 to be returned to the bank and
$450,000 for the lawyers. Pomerantz' share was only $60,000,
but that was more than three times what he had made in his
first ten years of practice.

The word spread. Soon Gertrude Bookbinder appeared with

her shares in the Chase Bank. The charges were not unlike those brought against National City. Chase settled for $2.5 million. This time Pomerantz received $150,000. As Tom Lehrer might have said, he was doing well by doing good. He had rediscovered the stockholder class action suit, which allows one lowly shareholder, owning as little as one share of stock, to question and to sue even the mightiest corporation—not in his or her own name, but in the name of all current and sometimes past stockholders. Pomerantz began to use this device to keep corporations in line. Somewhere along the way big business had forgotten that managers, presidents, and directors work for the shareholders, who are the true owners of the companies. Abe Pomerantz decided to make the stockholder suit his full-time business. How many people would come to wish he hadn't!

The lawyer was on his way. Little did he or any other mortal know then that his way would lead to his becoming the most frightening presence the securities business had yet encountered, a presence that would come to expose the rampant overcharging of the mutual fund industry and by so doing lead directly to the elimination of fixed brokerage commissions and the breakup of the private club that ran the New York Stock Exchange as an organization dedicated to the enrichment of its members at the expense of the general public.

But we're getting ahead of our story. It was to be a while before this David began slinging at the securities business and came to be known as a one-man substitute for the SEC. Other Goliaths needed to be brought down first—for example, William Randolph Hearst. In the 1930s Hearst had several money-losing newspapers on his hands. Not one to take his losses himself (it wasn't the American way), he formed a company called Hearst Consolidated Publications and sold his dogs to the company for a lot more than they were worth. Then he sold the company to the public, advertising in his own newspapers the preferred shares at $25 per. The unsuspecting public bought and then watched their share price erode to $8. Pomerantz brought suit, and the legend of San Simeon anted up $5 million.

After Hitler had come to power, a Wall Streeter visited Pomerantz bearing $450,000 in North German Lloyd bonds. The bonds were payable in marks, and now that the Nazis were in, those marks could be spent only in Germany and only for a few select purposes. Since North German Lloyd had changed the terms of the contract, the investor wanted out. And he wanted his money back in dollars.

The next week the steamship *Europa*, owned by North German Lloyd, docked in Brooklyn. Pomerantz got a sheriff, climbed on board, and attached the ship. Funny, how quickly the investor recovered his full $450,000. He told a friend, the friend told a friend, and a few days later Abe, armed with another client and another sheriff, climbed the gangplank of the *Bremen*. The client received $500,000. North German Lloyd had found that sailing to New York wasn't as much fun as it used to be.

While Pomerantz didn't care much for Hearst or the New York banks, he really disliked Krupp, Hitler's master armaments manufacturer. One day a refugee from Hitler's Germany arrived at his door bearing more than $1 million worth of Krupp bonds that he had managed to get out of Germany despite the Nazi decree that departing Jews could take no assets with them. Since a foreign company can't be sued in the United States unless it does business or has attachable assets here, Pomerantz had to send him away. But not for long. That evening he found at home a book about the Krupp empire. He stopped at the patent section. Sure enough, Krupp had licensed some patents to General Electric, which at that moment owed Krupp $440,000 in royalties. Moreover, General Electric's debt to Krupp was building at a rate of $100,000 a month. The client was recalled, and Pomerantz was able to collect the full principal amount of the bonds plus interest and costs, a total of $1,250,000. Nothing like curling up with a good book.

For a while Pomerantz dabbled in politics. In 1945 he ran for the New York State Supreme Court, but the electorate turned down his bid. That was probably a mistake. Had his candidacy been successful, however, who knows what tale we'd be writing today?

Instead of sitting on the bench, the would-be judge was sent to Nuremberg. His reputation as a trial lawyer who wasn't floored by the intricacies of financial transactions made him a natural to try the world's case against the German industrialists. But Pomerantz didn't stay there long. He got mad at the red tape, the Army, and Harry Truman; they were all dragging their feet. He quit, and he told the world all about it.

Back in New York, Pomerantz and his firm continued to be concerned with corporate abuses that were detrimental to stockholders. His cry became conflict of interest, his text the biblical admonition that no man can serve two masters. In these cases it was the stockholders versus the corporate managers themselves. It didn't hurt that somewhere along the way the courts had held that lawyers' fees in stockholder class actions should not be niggardly. In any one settlement, the individual stockholder might be reimbursed only some small amount of the total pie, but the lawyers should be well compensated in order to encourage them to keep the corporations in line.

Then came the 1960s, when every Wall Street secretary and president came to know a new name. Pomerantz attacked the mutual funds.

Mutual funds were established to let everyone, including the smallest investor, participate in the growth of American industry. The concept was simple enough: bring together lots of people, each with a modest amount of money. While no one individual would be expected to contribute enough to warrant the attention of a professional manager, the total subscriptions of hundreds or thousands of investors grouped together for a common investment cause would allow those investors to hire a professional to manage their money. The manager's fee would compensate him for his professional competence and whatever staff and research capability that would be required to make his investment judgments sound. In theory, the idea is not only good but socially beneficial: a way at last for the little guy to participate. In practice, it turned out to be a little different.

Mutual funds mushroomed in the 1950s. The recession that had been predicted to plague America following World War II never occurred. Soldiers who were supposed to return only to become unemployed as war production wound down instead came home to a new prosperity as American industry strove to rebuild what the war had destroyed. American savings, grown to record amounts with war rationing, grew even more as prosperity continued. Savings accounts bulged, and the public began looking for new areas in which to invest the accumulated surplus.

Not coincidentally, the New York Stock Exchange had recently begun a campaign to reawaken the public's interest in the securities markets. It figured, correctly, that memories were short and that most people who might have remembered the debacle of the Great Crash had either forgotten it or died. The public was rich, and getting still richer quickly once again seemed like a good idea. Most investors dealt directly with their brokers, but the more conservative (or less egotistical) liked the idea of the super professionalism of mutual funds. Wouldn't those funds have the very best managers? So they thought.

What the public did not know (and, you'll remember, no one was telling it) was that this was the era of fixed commission rates. With everyone back in the market, either individually or through mutual or pension funds, brokers were making out like bandits. While a good individual account might earn a broker a few thousand dollars a year, a good mutual fund account could generate hundreds of thousands of dollars a year in commissions. The mutual fund managers knew they had something to offer, and they wanted something in return. One thing they got, as we pointed out, was the creation of the institutional research brokerage house. These research firms wanted nothing to do with the individual investor. They turned out massive research on companies in which mutual funds might want to invest our money. In return for their research and analysis, they demanded and received the funds' commission business. It was a good deal for both sides; the research firms prospered, and the mutual fund managers didn't have to do the research they were being paid to do. They could fire their own analysts and keep the change.

The end of this gold-bricked road came in 1961. One of the mutual funds had gone too far. The case was *Lutz* v. *Boaz,* and it involved Managed Funds, a St. Louis-based mutual fund that managed some $80 million.

Over a six-year period Managed Funds had received $1.2 million in advisory fees from its fund shareholders. But it did little to earn those fees. Instead of managing the fund, the clever professionals turned the entire $80 million over to the firm of Model, Roland & Stone, a member of the New York Stock Exchange. Model, Roland actually ran the fund in return for 85 percent, more or less, of the commissions generated by the fund's transactions—a total of about $2 million before anyone got wind of what was going on. In doing so, Model, Roland "churned" the account; it bought and sold more than was necessary. In one year 97 percent of the "conservatively" managed fund was turned over.

The entire arrangement stank. The judge ruled it a flagrant abuse of the Investment Company Act of 1940 and assessed damages against Managed Funds and Model, Roland & Stone in excess of $1 million.

This was the stuff for Pomerantz. Where was the board of directors, the watchdog to protect shareholder interests? Theoretically, the mutual fund should be a separate entity from the management company that advises or runs it. And the law requires that at least 40 percent of the directors be "unaffiliated" (whatever that means). In the mutual fund business the manager *is* the fund. He hires the board of directors; he pays the retired generals $10,000 or $15,000 a year to watch over his shoulder. How many retirees would want to endanger that kind of added pension, particularly when you don't even have to show up for board meetings unless they are held in Hawaii or Aruba (all expenses paid of course). Independent my eye!

When was the last time an independent board of directors fired a manager for poor performance? Or even lowered his fee? Pomerantz decided to watch the watchdogs, and noticed that they weren't watching. They soon began to watch him.

It has been (and I suspect it remains) common for money managers to delegate their responsibilities to others. Toward the end of the 1960s Faulkner, Dawkins & Sullivan was a highly respected institutional research house. It had been one of the first to recognize the growing importance of the institutional investor. The three principals gathered around them the best research, sales, and finance people available and provided quality service to an ever-growing institutional clientele. Times have changed, and FD&S is now part of Loeb Rhoades Shearson. And Dwight Faulkner is now vice chairman of the second largest firm in the securities industry.

Dwight Faulkner was bright, aggressive, with all the usual attributes of a successful businessman. He tried to seek out the best people and then let them do their jobs in their own way, recognizing that one's own way, not his, allowed the individual's worth to be maximized. Sometimes he made a wrong choice, but not often. In its time Faulkner, Dawkins & Sullivan had one of the best research and sales teams ever assembled. And Faulkner did it.

One day there was a meeting in the FD&S offices. A grey-haired gentleman and his business adviser had come to talk money. They knew the firm's reputation, and they wondered whether the firm would manage a $2 million fund on a discretionary basis. The firm would make all the decisions for the account; its compensation would be the commissions generated. This was a typical arrangement for large accounts, and Faulkner, Dawkins could be trusted not to churn. The prospective client wanted only a detailed written quarterly report. Everyone shook hands.

A totally uneventful story. But it had another side. The new client had been in politics, had recently run for the wrong office and lost. Out of work! However, every good politician has a pocketful of IOUs, and this one had done lots of favors.

Now he needed one. Help came from a union official. Here was a $2 million union fund; here was a politician who knew zero about managing money. In the world of politics they made a perfect combination. The grey-haired man was being paid $40,000 a year out of union funds, just so someone could be nice to an old friend.

Now you can understand the significance of the detailed quarterly report requested. Every three months the Faulkner people would forward its statement. Unbeknownst to them, the statement was then retyped, verbatim, on the ex-politician's own letterhead (the one that said something about "investment advisory services"). And every three months the detailed report would go to the union fund trustees. It was always a good report, long and detailed and filled with the kind of Wall Street buzz words that inspire confidence in the unsophisticated. The arrangement lasted a number of years, and to this day those union members must be awfully impressed with the investment skills of a man who had devoted his life to clubhouse politics.

If Model, Roland and Managed Funds hadn't become greedy, maybe even Pomerantz might not have noticed the inventive ways in which mutual fund managers were spending their shareholders' money. But because they were greedy he did notice. One of the things he saw was the common practice of compensating with extra brokerage commissions the brokerage firms that sent customers to the mutual funds. The broker-dealers who sent the most business to any mutual fund received in return the most orders to buy or sell securities for that fund. In effect the advisers were paying a reward to any firm that helped to increase the fund's assets under management (and thereby the fund's advisory fees, which were based on a percentage of the assets).

There is nothing intrinsically wrong with that arrangement, providing that (1) the shareholders know what is going on with their money and (2) the participating broker is able to buy and sell securities for the fund at the best price. This is the area of execution capability. Suppose a fund wanted to buy

10,000 shares of IBM. Before the four-for-one split in 1979, that amounted to an order for roughly $3 million, give or take the odd $100,000. Some firms, even in the 1960s, specialized in finding large sellers for large buyers, and they might arrange a deal at $305 per share. Other firms, not having the right contacts, would just send the order to the floor of the New York Stock Exchange and hope for the best. The best might be an average price of $307 per share, in this case for a difference of $20,000 that would come out of the pockets of the fund's shareholders.

Pomerantz discovered that shareholders did not know what was going on and that often the brokers who were best at sending clients to mutual funds were not the ones who were best at executing orders. So, as was his wont, he brought suit. And this time he went to the very heart of the fund business: he attacked Mr. Johnson.

Edward C. Johnson II ran the Boston-based Fidelity Fund Group. In an industry noted for chumminess and first names, he was Mr. Johnson. People who had worked for him for forty years called him Mr. Johnson. He ran Fidelity while Lyndon Johnson was president of the United States. If someone in a brokerage office asked whether you knew what Johnson did or said, you knew he was talking about the Texan; if he asked whether you knew what Mr. Johnson did, you knew he meant Mr. Johnson.

In *Moses* v. *Burgin*, Pomerantz alleged that Mr. Johnson and his managers had not used their best efforts to save their shareholders brokerage commissions. By default they had used shareholder money to finance a sales effort. Mr. Johnson and the Fidelity managers settled out of court for $2 million.

Wall Street, and particularly the managers of institutional portfolios, went berserk. Of all the marbled pillars that held up the Wall Street establishment, Mr. Johnson was the most purely veined. And Pomerantz had had the nerve not only to haul him into court, but to win. Unthinkable! The SEC had been aware of these practices and had told the funds to cease and desist. Yet the funds had kept on with them until this guy from Brooklyn kicked them in their wallets. That's when it hurts.

Thus far Pomerantz and his firm have forced the mutual funds to return upward of $70 million to their shareholders. Recently he went to court again, accusing Dreyfus Liquid Assets of charging excessive fees.

We've already said that liquid asset funds may be the best thing (other than Abe Pomerantz) that ever happened to the small investor. But however good the fund idea was, Pomerantz didn't like the typical fee structure.

You don't have to be a genius to run these funds. The investments are so limited and well defined that almost any college graduate could learn all that's necessary in a week. Pomerantz thought that a fee of one-half of one percent was a little high, particularly when a single fund could be managing as much as $2 billion. In one four-and-one-half-year period Dreyfus had taken in $10 million in fees. Pomerantz got back 20 percent of that for the clients.

Beyond keeping mutual funds honest, or honester, Abraham Pomerantz single-handedly drew public attention to what everyone on Wall Street and at the SEC had known for years: that with research, kickbacks, reciprocity, and all sorts of other goodies, fixed commission rates had outlived any vestige of usefulness. In fact, fixed commission rates had died years before as the brokers vied with one another to see who could best satisfy any perceived institutional need at any cost. But the brokers and the institutions, for their own purposes, had kept the myth, if not the reality, alive.

Through the work Pomerantz did, the public learned the facts. And now fixed commissions are really dead—legally, in that anyone can negotiate the commission on any trade and practically, for with Abe Pomerantz looking over everyone's shoulder (or with everyone thinking he may be looking) no institution is going to give commission business to a friend without first checking that someone else out there might not be willing to do it for less. Today it's a simple question of dollars and cents. The brokerage firms are still doing research, and they are still being nice to their customers. They make up the difference a bit by outrageously overcharging the individual who is intimidated and loath to negotiate. But now the funds also have to look for the best prices, and a Wall Street era has ended. Most of the institutional research houses are gone, and seats on the New York Stock Exchange sell for a paltry $155,000 or so—a far cry from 1969, and the glory days of fixed rates, when a seat sold for $515,000. And that really wasn't so much, considering that the after-tax income of brokerage firms then averaged $150,000 a year per partner (and that of institutional firms, $337,000 per partner).

Pomerantz keeps threatening to retire but doesn't. Perhaps God's work is not yet done. Pomerantz still puts in longer hours than people half his age. Like the old lady who lives in the shoe with her oversupply of children, he almost has so many clients he doesn't know what to do next. We lunched the other day in his apartment overlooking Central Park. Of all the photographs in the apartment, he pointed out the one taken with Eleanor Roosevelt. We talked about his current work.

The themes are still conflict of interest and service to two masters. But the battleground has shifted to takeovers, friendly and unfriendly, and the conflicts that arise when one public company wants to buy out another—usually for a stock price substantially higher than that currently quoted on the exchanges.

One example was the recently aborted attempt by American Express to take over McGraw-Hill. In simple terms (there was nothing particularly complicated about it), American Express offered to buy McGraw-Hill for a cash price of $34 a share. When the board of directors rejected that offer, American Express raised the ante to $40 per share. Again the board refused. At the time of the offer, McGraw-Hill stock was selling on the New York Stock Exchange for $26 per share.

American Express had offered McGraw-Hill shareholders, through its offer to management and the board of directors, a premium of more than 50 percent on their stock. And the managers said no! So the American Express Company, conscious of its public image and unwilling to be branded as a raider, intruder, robber baron—you name it—packed up its moneybags and went in search of a warmer climate.

An irate stockholder of McGraw-Hill brought suit against his own board of directors and management. They had said no to $40 a share, and he was upset.

It is difficult to rationalize the reasons given by the board for refusing the American Express offer. They began by claiming that *Business Week* and other McGraw-Hill publications would lose their editorial independence. A reasonable consideration, but to my mind hardly a likely possibility; American Express didn't become the profitable giant it is by acting dumb. And to use *Business Week* as a house organ would be just plain stupid.

The board of directors and its lawyers also complained that McGraw-Hill had not invited the tender offer. Get that! It seems that the new American way requires a "for sale" sign before someone may express an interest. I own some woodland on Long Island. It's probably worth about $50,000 today, and it's just sitting there, with no sign to proclaim its salability. Imagine my response if someone should call to say that he had discovered that I owned the land and would like to pay me $75,000 for it. If I were to follow McGraw-Hill's example, I'd have to hang up on the guy after telling him that I don't accept windfall profits unless I solicit them.

Harold W. McGraw runs the publishing company. One may assume that he has sufficient wealth that he doesn't give much of a damn for a $40 or even a $34 offer for his company's stock. But is he aware that he and his family, some of whom have publicly come out in favor of the American Express offer, together own no more than 20 percent of the company's stock? That's quite a chunk, but that still leaves 80 percent in the hands of stockholders who were never given the chance to take part in the decision.

When the offer was announced, Harold McGraw went on a rampage. In advertisements in major newspapers he proclaimed that American Express "lacked integrity, corporate morality and sensitivity to professional responsibility." All them fighting words, just because a company had the gall to try to buy out—not steal, not kidnap, not terrorize—him and the other 80 percent.

I don't know how much heat will be put on Harold McGraw. But I'll go along with the *Barrons* editorial of February 5, 1979, written by Robert M. Bleiberg: "To Harold W. McGraw, Jr., a modest proposal: if you want a private fiefdom, buy out the other stockholders. At least let them choose." To that I'll add my own proposal to all of you who are McGraw-Hill stockholders (or if you find yourself in a similar situation): If you're happy as things stand, fine. If you're not and you aren't doing something about it, you have only yourselves to blame. When God sent Abe Pomerantz, he expected you to give him a little help.

I'm not suggesting that management should not fight offers from outsiders when they don't think them fair. But $40 a share is some 35 percent higher than McGraw-Hill stock has traded *at any time since 1970.*

It's difficult to believe that McGraw-Hill said no because it thinks the company is worth more than $40 per share. Since the market doesn't think so, it comes down to the question, did management say no because it believes the impossible or because it wanted to keep its jobs, its power, and its salaries? And did the independent board of directors—the protectors of the stockholders' interests—say no because it wanted to keep its perks? If Pomerantz has anything to say about it, they'll answer those questions in court before a public forum. Not a few other companies involved in mergers have already had to answer the same questions.

A while back Pomerantz was involved in the International Telephone and Telegraph Corporation's proposed merger with the Hartford Insurance Company. At that time IT&T didn't want to be dragged through the press and made to look like a bunch of bad guys. So it wrote a polite letter to the Hartford board of directors to say that it would like to buy the company for 80 percent more than its current market value. Hartford told IT&T to get lost. It would have, too, had not a Hartford shareholder, who also happened to be a client of Pomerantz' law firm, accidentally seen the IT&T letter. He raised cain! The board muttered something about thinking that the Justice Department wouldn't allow such a merger on antitrust grounds. The shareholder retorted that it was up to the government to bring suit—*after* the shareholders had been informed of the offer and been given a chance to accept or reject an 80 percent premium for their stock. The board disagreed, and the shareholder went to his lawyer.

Pomerantz wrote to each director. His letter isn't in the public domain, but one gathers that he likened each director of Hartford to a worker behind a delicatessen counter who, while the boss was out, received a customer who asked for a corned beef on rye and wondered whether the owner would take a check for twice the value of his deli. And the guy behind the counter, deciding for the owner (the shareholders), said no! (After all, maybe the new owner wouldn't like the way he cut the mustard.) It seems that Pomerantz included in his letter a little paragraph that said that if the board of directors did not reconsider the IT&T offer, he might be prepared to bring suit against Hartford, in the name of the shareholders, for $50 billion in damages. The merger suddenly went through very smoothly.

The government, by the way, did bring suit, claiming that the merger violated the antitrust provisions of the Clayton and Sherman acts. The government lost the case.

Certainly there are times when management should fight hard to prevent a takeover. Perhaps the classic case was the attempt of Leasco Data Processing Equipment Corporation to take over Chemical Bank. The 1960s was the era of the conglomerate. Saul Steinberg, the not yet thirty-year-old president of Leasco, had pulled off one of the biggest coups of the decade with Leasco's takeover of Reliance Insurance Company. In 1968 Leasco was a computer company with assets of $74 million, annual earnings of $1.4 million, and 800 employees. At that time it offered Reliance shareholders not cash (as American Express offered McGraw-Hill) but convertible Leasco de-

bentures and warrants for Leasco stock. On paper the deal
was worth more than the current price of the stock of the
old Philadelphia insurance company, and Reliance shareholders bit. Overnight Leasco acquired $350 million in annual reve-
nues and more than $100 million in capital that it could use
for further expansion. (That's one of the nice things about ac-
quiring insurance companies; they have all that lovely cash
flowing in from premiums.) The Reliance shareholders who
took Leasco's paper and immediately turned it into cash did
fine. Those who didn't did not.

Then Leasco set its sights high—too high. It got pushy. Imagine what it could do in the conglomerate game if it could take
over and control Chemical Bank—the $9 billion Chemical
Bank, the nation's sixth largest. Leasco made its move. It began
buying Chemical stock, and the financial community knew
something was up. It was expected that Leasco would offer
"wallpaper" (those same convertible bonds and warrants)
worth—again, on paper—some $110 per share for each share
of Chemical, which was then selling at $72.

Don't fight the big guys unless you can play in their league.
Reliance was small fish compared to Chemical Bank, and Saul
Steinberg was by no means an accepted member of the estab-
lishment. Chemical decided to treat impudence to a lesson.
Out came the guns and the school ties that fired them.

Chemical called its friends, the nation's other large banks.
Many of them sold all or most of the Leasco stock held in
their trust accounts, thereby forcing down the price of Leasco
and making its offer ever less attractive. Most large banks with-
drew or threatened to withdraw credit lines with Leasco. And
nearly every major bank made it known that it would not exchange any of its Chemical stock for Leasco paper. Defeated,
Steinberg crawled away. Chemical fought dirty, but the stakes
involved were not shareholder concerns alone but those of
banking as well. And bank monies must be treated in their
own special manner. (Besides, the offer wasn't for cash.)

The merger-nonmerger story is far from told. So take a hard
look the next time your company gets an offer. It may be a

bad one. Or it may come from American Express. Do yourself a favor; check it out. Pomerantz is probably out there doing it for you, but even he might miss one or two.

God seems to have picked the right man for the job. That one man has caused an entire country (and the government agencies who were supposed to do the job) to make corporations more concerned about their inside dealings; to force mutual funds to better serve their constituents; to make independent the independent board of directors; to end the arcane practice of fixed brokerage commissions; to make managements more aware of stockholder interests in merger situations; and to leave the securities industry with a sense of impending disaster should the fixed price of corporate underwritings be universally decried. (He's got a case pending on that last one now.)

How much more is there for him to do? God only knows. Maybe Abraham Pomerantz still has to make the world safe for nuclear energy, or to help stockholders in tobacco companies reap a bundle by decriminalizing marijuana. All we know for sure is that as long as he's around, and as long as there are walls and trumpets, walls will be a-tumbling down.

ACAPULCO GOLD

In 1972 the stock market passed the magic 1000 number on the Dow Jones Industrial Average. Almost every stock was up. Investors were happy; they loved to buy and sell. Brokers were happy. Mutual funds were especially happy. They didn't know what to do with the money piling up at their doors. They had invented funds for income, funds for growth, funds for speculation, funds for bonds, funds for funds. The public was in a buying mood, and Wall Street poured out the products.

Corporations were having a heyday, too. Expansion was the prevailing mood, and with stock prices going through the roof, companies were delighted to issue new stock at what they knew to be inflated prices. The public was buying anything. With the help of the Wall Street corporate finance departments, new forms of securities had recently gained popularity. Two of these were warrants and convertible bonds.

Warrants were usually little extras that were attached to the sale of new stock, often by very shaky corporations. The stock of companies that in less excited times wouldn't have been able to raise a dime was selling like hotcakes. Warrants gave the purchaser the right, along with his newly acquired 100 shares of PDQ Corporation, to buy, say, another 100 shares of PDQ within some fixed period of time. If he exercised the warrants, he would pay the same price for the additional stock that he had paid for his first 100 shares. Since everything was going up, and bodies in motion tend to stay in motion, what a break! Surely stock prices would double in a year, and he could then double his position at the original price. The public (and the institutions) ate it up.

They also ate up convertible bonds, a little device that seemingly gave investors the safety of bonds without sacrificing the growth potential of common stocks. Well, that's what we were told. In reality it didn't quite work that way.

An old saying holds that there is no such thing as a free lunch. But according to the hucksters of convertible bonds, lunch was on the house. Here was a $1,000 bond, paying interest and maturing (like any other bond) at a specific date. Unlike ordinary bonds, however, this one had a plus for the investor. The bonds could be converted at any time, at the option of the investor, into a stipulated number of shares of the corporation's common stock. Sounds like a free lunch, all right. Beware of Greeks. . . . If you had read further, you would have discovered that (1) the price of the corporation's common stock would perhaps have to double before the number of shares to which you could convert would equal your original $1,000 investment; (2) for the conversion privilege, the bond paid interest at a rate substantially below the prevailing rate for straight corporate debt; and/or (3) the underlying worth of the company was so insecure that the company couldn't raise money in the normal course of business and was therefore counting on an emotion-swept public to fall for gimmicks. In the last case, many ne'er-do-well corporations were aided and abetted by not a few Wall Street houses. No fraud, no lack of proper disclosure—just a reliance on an unsophisticated public's not taking the trouble to check. The old Trojan horse trick again!

Then, suddenly everything came to a screeching halt. The market turned around. After lingering at 1000 for a few days and encouraging pundits to predict 1200, 1300, even 2000 on the Dow, the market took a sustained downward course: 900, 850, 750, 600. By October 1974 it had hit 580.

Wall Street cut back. The limousines went; the charge accounts went; the first-class airplane seats went. It was survival time. Investors had gone into hiding; corporations had stopped raising money; the public had withdrawn from the mutual funds. The institutions stood with their mouths open, powerless by virtue of their size to do anything but watch the value of their clients' "glamour issue" portfolios tumble along with the rest of the market. People who ran mutual funds took up farming, and brokers lined up for hack licenses.

There was gloom in the Street. Lots of firms folded. But those that survived got busy. Busy is business.

The question in every boardroom was, What could bring the investor, and his fee-paying money, back?

"When the going gets tough . . ."—and Wall Street is tough. It knew that investors would come back eventually; they always did. But how to get them back sooner rather than later? Wall Street needed a new gimmick—something to show the investor that this time it was different, this time it was safe. When the mutual funds bellyed-up like everything else, something new, something confidence-inspiring had to be found. But what?

Options, that's what. And did they ever catch on! For as long as anyone can remember, options had been available to investors through a few over-the-counter houses. No one had paid much attention to them. They were for the sophisticates and the gamblers, and the Street had had so many other things to sell. Now one of the oldest games in town was dusted off and proclaimed the newest game in town. We are not yet certain what it has done for investors, but it sure saved a lot of brokerage firms.

An option is a contract made between a speculator and someone who owns common stock in a corporation. For a price (the cost of the option contract) the owner of the stock agrees to sell to the speculator a set number of shares (usually a multiple of 100 shares) at a prearranged price anytime within a specified period of time, typically three, six, or nine months.

The speculator is betting that the price of the stock will go up in that period of time. For example, suppose that XYZ Corporation is selling today at $100 a share. Rather than plunk down $10,000 for 100 shares of XYZ, the speculator may find someone who, for a fee of only $500, will agree to sell his own 100 shares of XYZ within the next three months at a price of $100 per share. (Obviously, the current owner will be someone who doesn't share the speculator's belief that XYZ is about to take off.)

Now here's the basis of option speculating. If XYZ goes to 110, the speculator will exercise his option. He will pay the owner of the stock $10,000 and then resell the stock at its current market price of $11,000. The speculator actually paid out $500 and got $1,000 back. He doubled his money, even though the value of the stock of XYZ Corporation increased only 10 percent from 100 to 110. That's financial leverage. The option buyer did all right for himself.

If XYZ went to 110 before the option expired, the speculator could get out early by finding someone to buy his option from him. Since the option would allow the new owner to buy $110 stock for $100, the option itself had increased in value. Why then cast him as a speculator? Well look a little further. Suppose XYZ increased only to 105 during the option period. The speculator who paid $500 for the option would then buy the stock for $10,000 and sell it for $10,500. He paid in $10,500 and took out $10,500: zero rate of return.

It gets worse. Suppose that XYZ doesn't move. It just stays at 100. No reason to exercise that option now. The speculator has lost $500. Now, $500 in itself isn't so much, but it amounts to 100 percent of the speculator's investment. And he's lost it all. That's the other side of financial leverage: it magnifies profits, but it also magnifies losses. A lot of $500 losses can mount up.

In this example the speculator begins to make money when XYZ moves above 105. He loses (because he paid $500 for the option) when XYZ is between 100 and 105. If XYZ remains at 100 or falls below, he loses 100 percent of his investment. That's why he's a speculator.

It's a different story for the owner of the stock, the option seller. He owns $10,000 worth of XYZ. He sells an option and pockets $500. Now if XYZ goes to 110, well too bad. He will get $10,000 from the speculator in addition to the original $500. At least he has a 5 percent profit. If XYZ stays at 100, he will still have his stock plus an extra $500 profit without his stock having moved. And if XYZ falls below 100, that extra $500 will help to cushion his paper loss while he waits for better days. (As he waits, he can sell a new option contract each time the old one expires.) Thus the seller of options is usually a conservative investor. He owns the underlying stock and, through the sale of options, tries to modestly increase the income his portfolio generates.

So options buyers are speculators and options sellers are cautious conservatives who are not interested in the big killing. Well, that's the way it used to be. But Wall Street, in pursuance of its latest game, has mixed the dice and cast them in such a way as to make it difficult to tell the little old ladies from the hard-core gamblers. We'll see how.

Before 1973, options were arranged rather informally by a handful of brokerage firms that specialized in what had been an obscure offshoot of the principal securities business. Option buyers would go to those firms and state their preferences. They could freely arrange the date on which an option would expire and the number of shares to contract for. The firm would then try to find a seller (or become one itself), and expiration dates and numbers of shares in the contract would be negotiated. In this tailor-made market, the options created were usually held until expiration date and were not readily marketable.

One day in April 1973 all this changed. The Chicago Board of Trade launched the Chicago Board of Options Exchange. Without much fanfare, options began to be listed, quoted, and traded in one central marketplace. The label "Overnight Success" doesn't begin to describe the resulting explosion. Suddenly options had a national focus. The CBOE (and the other exchanges that followed its example) standardized options: the size of an option contract was made uniform (100 shares); expiration dates were set at three-month intervals, with option lives available for three, six, or nine months (on the date that one option contract expires, a new one is established); and strike prices were made uniform (e.g., the CBOE listed three separate options for Eastman Kodak, all of which expired in April 1979: one at a strike price of 50, a second at 60, a third at 70). Obviously, the prices of option contracts with such different strike prices will be substantially different, depending on the current market price of the underlying stock and the amount of time remaining before the option expires.

On that day in April 1973 the CBOE listed options for the common stock of sixteen corporations. In its first full month of activity the CBOE moved 54,134 contracts. Today this figure represents less than one hour's activity on the exchange. In all of 1973 only 1.1 million contracts were sold. Then Wall Street brokers caught on and began educating their customers. Volume grew to 5.6 million in 1974.

The American Stock Exchange, recognizing a good thing, began listing options in 1975, soon to be followed by the Philadelphia, Pacific, and Midwest exchanges. The battle for the dual listing of options became intense, particularly between the CBOE and the American Stock Exchange. Just how intense was recently underscored by an article in the *Wall Street Journal* detailing how a group of young men working on the Chicago Board were busted for dealing in cocaine, a commodity for which there is as yet no publicly listed market. The arrest caused one Wall Street insider to muse that this may have been the only time that the Amex did not push for a dual listing. It also caused an unnamed member of the SEC to remark that until the police moved in, the above mentioned market had been the most orderly and well conducted on the CBOE.

In June 1977 the New York Stock Exchange announced plans to get in on the action. But it had finally occurred to the SEC that trouble might be brewing. Since 1973 options volume had grown 5,000 percent. The SEC issued an order freezing new options listings until it could study complaints of trading abuses. The study will probably go on for years.

Meanwhile, options for 202 companies have been listed on various exchanges and trading has become frantic: In April

1978 the New York Stock Exchange traded a record-breaking 63.5 million shares of common stock (compared to a mere 16.4 million shares traded on Black Tuesday, October 29, 1929). Hardly noticed on the evening news report that same day was that options contracts representing more than 65 million shares had also been traded. Even with the freeze on new options listings, it was estimated that the volume of options trading would be up 33 percent in 1979. Never had a new game caught on so quickly; everyone was playing, including bank trusts and pension funds. And they're playing while the SEC is investigating. Investigating what?

The phenomenal increases in trading volume have caused trouble. In September 1978 one specialist firm on the American Stock Exchange suffered such heavy losses in its own dealings in the options of Bally Manufacturing that it had to receive emergency financial aid to stay afloat. Had the firm gone under, how long would it have taken for the small investor to get his account straightened out? The same question might be asked of any Wall Street firm.

More frightening, the SEC has censured and fined several options specialists (the people who make a market in listed options) on the American Stock Exchange. The specialist is a member of the brokerage community who is little known to the investing public; under current trading conditions, he is an integral part of the investment process.

Every security, including options, that is listed on an exchange is doled out to a particular specialist. When we give our broker an order to buy IBM, that order is transmitted by our broker to his representative on the floor of the New York Stock Exchange. That representative in turn goes to the booth of the specialist who handles IBM. There, literally surrounding the specialist, are all the brokers who hold orders to buy or sell IBM—our orders, institutional orders. In an active market, or in an active stock, the specialist sits back and lets the representatives of the buyers and sellers offer and accept among themselves.

The specialist may join in the activity in any of three ways.

First, he may buy or sell the security for his own account, in effect like any other investor. Second, he keeps what is known as the "limit order book." Suppose I put in an order to buy IBM at 65 when IBM is trading at 70. When I put in the order, my broker doesn't laugh me out of the office. We both know that my order won't be filled—not yet, that is. My order is transmitted to the floor of the exchange and entered in the specialist's limit order book. I have put a limit on my order instead of ordering "at the market." When and if IBM falls to 65, the specialist will check the book and buy 100 shares for me at or below 65. Third, the specialist maintains orderly markets. Essentially this means that if I want to buy or sell a listed security in which there may not be very much activity, the specialist is required to buy from me or to sell to me, from his own inventory, some limited number of shares at a price near the previous close if no buyer or seller can be found to match my order.

The SEC censured those American Stock Exchange specialists for rigging option prices. And we all thought that that kind of stuff had gone out when the SEC came in in 1934. No, sir. Worse, the firms admitted their guilt and with enviable hauteur claimed that they were acting in the public interest to maintain orderly markets.

Options prices usually move in tandem with the price of the underlying common stock. If Kodak stock is selling at 57, for example, options expiring in two months with a strike price of 60 may be selling for $2. If Kodak stock goes quickly to 65, the value of the option may go to $6 or $8. Thereafter, a dollar increase in the stock usually results in a dollar increase in the price of the option, particularly if the stock is already selling above the option strike price. This is the option holder's dream situation; it provides the real leverage in options.

What the censured specialists were doing was simple enough: At or near the closing of the exchange each day, they would check the price at which a particular option was trading. If the specialists thought the price of an option was too low (relative to the price of the underlying stock), they put in a fictitious order for an option contract at a higher price, and that price became the option's closing price for the day. It also usually became the price at which the option opened the next morning—the price at which they happily sold you contracts from their own inventory if you were an unwitting early morning buyer.

American Stock Exchange officials knew that their members were clearly acting illegally, but pushed hard on the argument that it was being done only to maintain orderly markets. And the SEC, the knight of right, guardian of the faithful, entity of the United States government dedicated to protecting the big and the little from fraudulent investment practices, went along with the exchange. It gently slapped the wrists of the price fixers and told them not to do it again. Similar activities a few years back on the part of some guys at Westinghouse and General Electric (not with securities but with electrical apparatus) sent those guys to prison.

A host of violations have been alleged against members of the Chicago Board. The massive volume of transactions has caused paperwork foul-ups and the mismatching of orders, but these are only procedural problems, and they are seemingly being cleared up. Meanwhile, one wonders whether rigging and disorganization have cost the exchanges—or did the unwitting customer end up paying for them?

Certainly one little trick always seems to cost the small investor. That is the calling of "fast markets," a device by which specialists close their limit order books (that is, discontinue transactions) pending a more orderly market. "Fast markets" usually means that an institution's trades will go through but those of the small investor will not. Once again, even when the small investor is smart enough to take his profits or to limit his losses, insider fooling around may limit his ability to do so.

Supposedly the SEC is also investigating the relationship between options prices and the prices of the underlying stocks to see whether movements in stock prices influence options prices. That should be the case, but strange things seem to happen. The SEC knows that some funny business is going on, but, like relativity, no one has yet been able to see it. It has a name, though. It's called "capping."

Capping is an underhanded practice engaged in by large institutional sellers of options. When an option is due to expire and the stock is moderately above the strike price (and therefore likely to be called away), these large holders of the underlying stock are believed to be guilty of dumping large blocks of the stock on the market, momentarily lowering the price of the stock and thereby keeping it from being called. After the option has expired, they buy back their stock and continue on their option-selling way. Nice work if you can get it.

Consider again the small investor. Even when he knows he is speculating by buying options in the first place, the wheel is being fixed in ways he could never think to calculate. Wall Street plays its games seriously, sometimes so well that neither you nor I—nor, seemingly, the SEC—knows who is in there playing. (If the SEC does know, so far it has seen no reason to tell us.)

On the good side, the current competition, principally between the CBOE and the American Stock Exchange, represents the first real competition that has ever existed in the securities business. At present the CBOE trades 95 options on underlying stocks, and the American Exchange trades 64. (Significantly, ten issues are common to both.) If and when the New York Stock Exchange, with its mammoth influence on the securities business, enters the competition, the ensuing competitive environment may well work in the investor's favor. Yet even then there may be a hitch. If the NYSE is allowed in, it will be easy for brokers to use the NYSE for one-stop shopping. The brokers will like the convenience, and unless we are large accounts, they may put that convenience ahead of our right to obtain the best price.

At any rate it's time for a closer look.

We need to examine both sides of the options business, the selling and the buying. Traditionally, as we've said, option sellers have been conservative investors and option buyers speculators. But, as in most of Wall Street's games, there are different ways to play. 1977 was a pretty flat year for the stock market. President Carter was new to office. He had lots of good intentions, but the public knew that the road to hell had always been paved with good intentions. The stock market was waiting, so 1977 became a good year for selling options in conservative accounts.

Sears, Roebuck is a good, solid company. In 1977 it was selling for about $23 a share and paying $1 a year in dividends (a return of about 4 percent on the current price). We didn't expect Sears to do very much one way or the other in that waiting market, so we sold options against the stock our clients held. We sold three-month options at a strike price of 25 for $2 ($200 per contract for each 100 shares). Sears didn't reach 25, so our customers just took in that extra income.

When the contracts expired, we sold new ones on the same stock. There were small fluctuations in the market price of Sears, down to 22, up to 24. Sometimes the price of the option was a little above $2, sometimes a little below, but $2 was about average. In all, we sold options four times in 1977 and took in a total of $8 for each share we held. Since each share also earned $1 in dividends, our customers collected a total of $9 per share that year, and they still owned their stock. In a year in which the stock market hardly moved and Sears stayed at about 23, our customers made about 39 percent on their money—not a bad return by most standards.

We did the same thing with a few other blue-chip companies. Sometimes, even in that dull market, the price of the stock moved momentarily above the strike price. Rather than have the stock called away, we bought the contracts back and sold new ones at a higher strike price. We gave back some of the gains that way, but in general we did all right, mainly because we concentrated on blue chips that could be expected not to have any big price gyrations.

When March 1978 came around, the dollar firmed on the international currency exchanges and that dull stock market took off like a bat. Options selling was no longer the right strategy. We quit selling options, held on to the stocks, watched them go up a few points, and then got the hell out. The stock market scared us. It was going crazy—up crazy, but crazy nonetheless. The dollar wasn't acting very well, inflation was stampeding, Carter was talking about recession, and we weren't sleeping well. Out!

Sure, we could have kept on selling options. But what comfort would those few dollars have been if the $23 stocks we held on to fell to $12? Treasury bills yielding 9½ percent gave us and our customers sweet dreams. This time we were right, and our very conservative philosophy produced some very unconservative profits. We dealt in conservative stocks, and we were willing to change strategies when it seemed right.

But remember, 202 options are listed on the Chicago Board and other exchanges. A lot of those 202 companies aren't as solid as Sears. In 1977 Bill Marshall was doing very well in options. His broker had gotten him interested and had worked out an investment program for him. But the broker wanted his client to do *really* well. Instead of companies such as Sears, he bought Sambo's Restaurants and National Semiconductor for Mr. Marshall. These stocks fluctuated much more widely than our conservative stalwarts, and greater volatility meant higher call premiums. National Semiconductor stock could move (up or down) more in a week than Sears would in a year.

Mr. Marshall did very well in 1977, better than any of our clients. But then came 1978. He still did well as the market began to climb. But his stocks rose above the strike price and they all got called away. No problem; the broker bought them again at higher prices and sold new options. By hanging on to the old strategy Marshall was still doing O.K., but not as well as he would have been doing in a savings bank. Then came the crash. As quickly as the Dow Jones Average had gained 100 points in the first half of the year, it lost it in the second half. Our friend's stocks tumbled. Sambo's, bought at 20, was sold at 10, and all his other holdings experienced similar declines. In six months Mr. Marshall gave back more than he had made in the previous year and a half. Once again, the familiar story: he changed his broker, but it was a little too late. I doubt that the broker was nearly as greedy as he was stupid. Options have their time and place. For the conservative investor, selling options can be safe—at the right time. And if you, or those you rely on, can't figure out when that is, keep away.

It may not appear that way, but Mr. Marshall was one of the more fortunate players in 1978. At least his broker didn't suggest that he go naked. Going naked doesn't mean quite what you may think it does, but it may involve your losing your shirt.

A naked option is one that you sell without owning the stock against which that option is written. Perfectly legal. You think a stock will fall or at least not go up to the strike price. In the Sears example, you sell an option at 25 when the stock is at 23. You take your $200 without owning the stock. If the price is below 25 when the option expires, you make $200 without having put up a dime. But if the stock shoots up to 30—not likely with Sears, but ever so easy with National Semiconductor—you will have to buy the stock at 30 ($3,000) and deliver it at 25 ($2,500). You have lost ($500 − $200) $300. For speculators, that may just be part of a day's work; for the conservative investor, it's disaster. But, you protest, no conservative investor would do anything like that; going naked doesn't sound prudent. Don't forget the emperor and his new clothes. Wall Street has a way of making naked appear fully dressed. Here you need bring together only two elements: a greedy broker and an unwary investor.

Of course, no broker in his right mind would talk to a conservative investor about naked options. Suppose, however, that a client owns Sears, or even National Semiconductor, and sells options against his holding. Picture the happy client making money without his stock moving! Then comes a suggestion from the broker: "How about making twice as much money? Since your National Semi is not moving anyway, and the options you've sold against your 100 shares have brought you some income, why not sell options against 200 shares?" Such a dirty word as naked is never used.

A client in the 1977 market makes a bundle; his stock doesn't move, the strike price is never met, the income for his account doubles. And not bad for the broker, who is doubling up on commissions. Then comes the big rally of 1978. By this time the broker has you selling 5 options against your 100 shares. National Semi moves from 15 to 35 before you know what business they are in. Naively, you might be pleased that your $15 stock has more than doubled. But don't plan that vacation yet. The fact is that your 100 shares have been called away at 20. That's not bad. But the other 400 shares have also been called away at 20—the 400 shares you don't own. Fooled you; you were naked all the time! You now have to buy 400 shares at 35 ($14,000) and then sell them immediately at 20 ($8,000). You've lost a cool $6,000 before you knew what was happening.

The numbers don't really mean much. Depending on your portfolio, they could be larger or smaller. In this example, a $6,000 loss isn't much for a speculator when considered against the possible gains. The real question is, were you a speculator? If you intended to be, that's the way the game is played. But if you thought you were a conservative risk avoider, you were had. And it's no good complaining afterward that you were deceived. People who write options must sign papers that say they know or have had explained to them what they are doing. If you didn't read the fine print, that's your problem. But you've got company: Hundreds of thousands of investors, conservative, income-oriented investors, offices full of bored, retired investors in retirement communities around Miami, Phoenix, and Palm Springs are often drawn unwittingly into this new game. And too many don't realize they can't afford to play.

It's those investors—and you, if you are one of them—that I am concerned about. Many people in this country enjoy their current standard of living due in part to the income generated from their portfolios. If they use options as a part of a conservative, well-structured investment strategy, fine. They can rely on that structure to gain additional spending money or for inflation protection through the sale of options. In a well-thought-out, carefully followed program, they or their advisers would follow closely the market price movements of the underlying stocks against which options have been sold. And these stocks would not be Bally Manufacturing, National Semiconductor, or any other widely fluctuating, high-flying, fast-moving hot issue. Rather, they will be what we euphemistically call blue chips. When they begin to make upward moves, the portfolio strategy would call for options to be bought back at certain points so that the underlying stock, and its dividend yield, will not be called away. You may have to give back the premium you received for selling the option, but your income and your standard of living are protected.

But often this doesn't happen. Strategies are not clearly thought out and brokers too often are guilty of supporting or encouraging investor greed. Consider a hypothetical case: Suppose our retired investor has assembled a portfolio with a value of $200,000. That portfolio should not be subjected to large amounts of risk. (Recall the performance of National Semiconductor.) If that portfolio contains a diversified group of companies such as Sears, DuPont, and General Motors, it might yield today some $15,000 in dividends. Options can and often should be sold to increase that income. However, each of those stocks is currently thought to be low-priced. With some good economic news and a sustained bull market, each could double in price. Our retired investor, if not cautioned to buy back the options he has sold, may suddenly find all his securities called away. Small comfort those option premiums he's banked when he suddenly discovers that he can now buy only half the number of shares he previously held (and then receive only half the dividend income he previously enjoyed). This example may seem extreme, but it can and does happen. Remember, the psychological makeup of the unsophisticated investor who sees his stocks move down in price often leads him to assure himself that they will go up again. How many investors, when they see their stocks rise above their option strike prices, will employ a variation of that same psychology and ask, Why give back those nice option premiums? Surely my stocks will come down again.

One could also argue that if you can't stand the heat, you ought to get out of options. But that assumes too much rationality. Most investors have to be carefully led, hand in hand, by those who know better.

That brings us to Catch-22. Those who are most often perceived as knowing better are brokers. And brokers have their own bills to pay. Too much good advice from them could put their kids right back into the public schools. So perhaps we can't blame them too much when an option-hungry public pleads to be let in on the action. Maybe that's why they invented "spreads." Now there are bull spreads, bear spreads, and time spreads in the options business; each of them is designed to limit a conservative investor's risk of loss. Together, these spreads are known to the trade as Acapulco spreads.

In a bull spread you expect a stock to move up in price. For example, you buy the Boeing May 70s at a price of $4 ($400 for the contract). To reduce the cost, however, you simultaneously sell the May 80s, which might be fetching $1 ($100 for the contract). Therefore your May 70s, on which you expect to make money, really cost you only $300. If the stock goes to 80, your May 70s are worth $10 and the poor guy you sold the 80s to has worthless paper. Above a stock price of 80, what you lose on the 80s you make up on the 70s. Therefore, on such a bull spread as this, you can't lose more than $300 and you can make as much as $700 ($1,000 less the $300 cost).

Bear spreads are just the opposite. You expect the stock to go down in price, so you sell the 70s and buy the 80s. On calendar spreads you may buy Boeing May 70s and sell Boeing August 70s.

Because of their limitation on risk (as well as reward) spread options have been very successfully sold to conservative investors who want to have a little fun.

But I've left out one minor detail. Every time you do a spread trade, you are simultaneously making two trades, a purchase and a sale. Therefore you pay your broker two commissions.

When it's time to unwind your position, you turn around and sell what you bought and buy what you sold: again, two trades, and again, two commission charges. That's why brokers call them Acapulco spreads. After deducting commissions, the customer, if he's been a bull when he should have been, or a bear when he ought, still doesn't make very much profit. And if he beared when he should have bulled or Mayed when he should have Augusted, he loses money. But bull or bear, summer or fall, the broker has made enough on commissions to take the wife and kids to Acapulco every winter weekend. Hasta luego.

In contrast, option selling by professional institutional managers of conservatively run accounts has proved to be a worthwhile tool. Of course, the institutional managers don't have to pay the exorbitant commissions that you pay. Options have been used with great success by, among others, the managers of the City of Memphis' Light, Gas & Water Division's retirement fund.

The fund's managers recognize that writing covered options is a way to reduce susceptibility to downward stock movements while at the same time providing extra income in periods of rising stock prices. They are willing to lock in smaller profits in good times and to play against downside risks in bad. And considering the performance of most pension funds, they seem to be on the right track. Of course with the fund's assets in the hundreds of millions, and with continuous supervision, the fund's managers are not in the same position as our hapless retiree who occasionally wanders into his broker's office or calls every now and then when rain keeps him off the golf course.

What the Memphis fund does is buy a stock, one it respects, and simultaneously write an option on it, usually one with a strike price *below* the stock's current market value. For this they receive a sizable option premium. They fully expect the stock to be called away, but they have a locked-in profit that makes them smile. They seem to have learned that greed, historically, does not pay.

The result: the Memphis fund grew from $52 million in 1975

to $85 million at the end of 1977. Only $10 million of that increase represented additional contributions. In 1978, a year in which the Dow Jones Industrial Average made no net change, the fund was up another 9 percent. Not many pension funds can match that performance. Perhaps more of the high-priced money managers should put their egos aside and follow the Memphis example.

Back to us ordinary investors. If you've sold options or are thinking about doing so, don't pack up and quit. Options can give you additional income and that's not bad. But they should be a part of a well-planned program and only one part of a diversified portfolio. And they should be watched. The option egg is not as hard-boiled as it's often made out to be. It can crack.

The other side of the option game, buying options, is strictly for gamblers. It's an all-or-nothing proposition: you make a bundle or lose the entire ante.

A while back the *Wall Street Journal* told the spectacular story of a man who made some $4 million by buying Boeing options. Boeing stock had been depressed for a long time. The government had cut back on aerospace spending, and the airlines already had too many planes. Then the CAB relaxed the rules on air fares, big discounts on seats were instituted, and the airlines were doing better than ever. They needed Boeing again, and the orders poured in. Our man saw it coming. He put everything he had into Boeing, not into the stock but into options. He knew he could lose it all, but if he was right, he could retire for life. Not many of us are or should be willing to take such a risk, particularly when, as with options, you not only have to be right but you have to be right within a specific period of time. Unless you're using only your gin rummy money, you need ice water in your veins to play in this ball park.

The guy made a bet and doubled his money; then he let it ride. Boeing began 1978 at 26. The iceman put everything into Boeing 25s. When the stock price went up, he sold the 25s at a profit and put everything into the 30s. That's called pyramiding. Boeing kept going up. Every dime of his profits from the 30s went into the 35s, then into the 40s, the 45s, the 50s. And on into the 60s, the 70s, and the 80s. Then he quit. Boeing got up to 80 and then started going down. Had he stayed in three seconds longer he would have lost it all. Simple: The odds were a billion to one against him. He took them, and he won.

A more typical story is that of the kid who worked in a drugstore. He walked into a broker's office one day, plunked down $800, and said he wanted to play options. He came up against a responsible broker who took the trouble to find out that the $800 represented the twenty-two-year-old's life savings. The broker suggested that it might be a good time to start buying some life insurance. "Low rates at your age." He'd hear none of it. "Perhaps a few shares of some good, solid stock?"

"Cut the crap," the kid intoned. "Its Vegas, OTB, or options." The broker called his office manager, decided the kid was sane, and accepted the account.

"O.K.," the kid said, "What do I buy?" Here comes Boeing again. It was March 1978, and the manager suggested 4 Boeing May 25 options. The kid started making money. He did exactly what our other hero did: he kept pyramiding, following the advice of the office manager, who just happened to know something about stocks and options. Within five months his $800 had grown to $60,000. He got married, took out $10,000 to furnish an apartment, went on the night shift at the drugstore— and got cocky. He kept heeding the manager's advice; he diversified into Tiger International and Syntex options, and he kept making money. He had found a good broker, and he stuck with him.

Then came September 1978. The broker didn't like the market, and he told the kid it was time to quit the options market. "Don't be a fool," said the instant expert. Even good brokers are only brokers; they don't have the power to take children over their knees. The kid bought October, November, and December options. All expired worthless. He lost every penny.

Last we heard, he still had his furniture and was subscribing to any service offered on gold. He decided that gold will sell at $500 an ounce within twelve months. Right again. But did he get out or will it be $1,000 or nothing? We'll see.

The kid did well initially because he started in a rising market; when stocks are going up, buying options can magnify your profits. But you've got to know when to quit. He didn't. The record shows that most individuals—and most professionals—don't know either. So I caution: Casinos and gambling can be fun, particularly when you decide that you'll play only with an amount of money that you can afford to lose. Then, if you win, you can tell your friends for months about your system and they'll all envy your smarts. Same with buying options. If you lose, chalk it up to an evening's entertainment. Even the conservative investor needs a little fun, and buying options every now and again can be a kick. Just make sure that you buy with that small portion of your portfolio that you can afford to lose. Then it's rather like the casino. Otherwise, the only sure winner is the broker, who gets his kicks while you get pummeled.

One more story to end a chapter about options on an uptick:

Three institutional salesmen, working for the same major New York Stock Exchange firm but in different offices around the country, spoke to each other almost every day to compare notes. Each decided to put some money into options, and Boeing was their choice. In June 1978 they all bought the Boeing August 50s. On the Quotron machine (the computer you hit to get current prices) the symbol for those options was BAHJ. Each of the salesmen made $12,000 profit on that particular investment, each got out and each put his profits into identical white BMWs. But only one of them lived in a state that allowed license plates with letters alone, and he now drives the California freeways in his spanking bright car, bearing on its tail plate forever his fondest stock market memory—B A H J!

THIS LITTLE PIGGY
WENT TO MARKET

Once upon a time there was a sweet young married couple living poorly in Manhattan. They lived poorly because they had no money. He wanted to do better things, but he only drove a taxicab. She kept house. She could have worked, but it wouldn't fit into our story.

Mike came home every night and talked about that one big break. Barbra listened and wanted to be helpful, but there was nothing she could do. So they took a lotta baths together.

One evening Mike came home flushed with excitement. One of the men at the cab company had let him in on a sure thing. The Russians were coming to the United States—not with bombs, with money. Money to buy pork bellies. Frozen pork bellies, whence comes bacon. With the Russians in the market the price of pork bellies was bound to go up, and a smart speculator could make a fortune. Mike wanted to be rich, and he needed only $3,000. That was the margin requirement for buying contracts for pork bellies on the commodities exchange. Just $3,000 would buy him $60,000 worth of pork bellies. And at 56 cents a pound, every one-cent increase in the price of bellies would give Mike a profit of $1,071. Of course, a drop in price of less than 3 cents would wipe Mike out, but the cabbie had said that the Russians were definitely coming—it was a sure thing. Mike's big break was here at last.

Mike looked at Barbra, and Barbra looked at him. They didn't have $3,000. Mike was disappointed, and Barbra felt bad. So they took a bath and went to bed. But Barbra couldn't sleep. She had to get the money for Mike, just for a few days so that he could make his killing. Mike was such a good person; he deserved to be rich. But where to get the money? All night Barbra thought.

The next morning, after Mike had left for work, Barbra called all her friends and relatives—and came up empty. She tried the banks; nothing. She tried the building superintendent; he didn't have $3,000 to lend. But, the superintendent said, there was always Louie the Loanshark. And Barbra was desperate.

Louie the Loanshark had the money, at 10 percent a week. Barbra didn't care. In a few days they'd be rich. Louie gave her the money and said she didn't have to sign anything. He knew where to find her. That evening Barbra gave Mike the bankroll and told him she'd gotten it from her cousin in Texas. Mike was very happy; Barbra was happy, too. They took another bath.

In the morning Mike called a broker and went long pork bellies. At last they'd found the better way.

Days went by, then a week. There was no movement in pork bellies, neither up nor down. Where were those damned Russians? Mike began to worry. Barbra worried even more.

She tried to explain to Louie the Loanshark about the pork bellies and the Russians. Just a few more days. Louie wasn't sympathetic. He sent some guys in a car to run Mike over. They didn't get Mike because he was young and athletic and ran pretty fast. But Barbra was scared; she knew trouble. She worried so much she couldn't even take a bath.

The next day she went to see Louie. She told him again about the Russians and how pork bellies couldn't miss. Louie said *he* wouldn't miss—unless Barbra found someone to buy her contract.

The superintendent who had been so helpful came through again. Maybe Mollie the Madam? Anything, Barbra said.

Mollie the Madam bought Barbra's contract from Louie for $4,000. All Barbra had to do was to call Mollie when Mike left for work. Then Mollie would send Barbra some nice John to play with. A little "at home" service bureau. Barbra would do anything for Mike.

The first customer was a judge. He fell and cracked his skull chasing Barbra around the apartment. The second was a very respectable businessman who had a heart attack when Mike came home for lunch. Mollie the madam knew a bad thing when she saw one, and she decided to cut her losses. She sold Barbra to some hit men for $5,000.

This time the work would be easier. Barbra need only wear a wig and deliver some packages. Like bombs to blow people up. Sure enough, she couldn't do that right either. She blew up the hit men's trailer.

For $6,000 Barbra was sold to a cattle rustler. Her new assignment was to drive a truck filled with stolen bulls from New Jersey to New York. Somewhere in Brooklyn Barbra hit a car and all the bulls ran down DeKalb Avenue. Barbra went to jail. Now Mike would find out the whole story. They had taken their last bath together. Barbra was very sad.

Enter Mike. That's right; the Russians had finally arrived. Pork bellies were up. Mike was rich. He forgave Barbra everything, and they moved to an apartment with two bathrooms and lived happily ever after. Just like in the movies.

Just like in the movies because this *is* a movie—it's a rough scenario of *For Pete's Sake,* a not so terrific Barbra Streisand vehicle of a few years back, Hollywood's version of the commodity futures market. In Hollywood the good guys always win, even in commodities. That's what Hollywood is all about; it's not supposed to be real life.

Real life in commodities speculating is the flying trapeze without a net. A guy could get killed—financially. And guess whom Wall Street is now pitching this game to. Come back Mike and thousands like him.

In the United States commodity trading is conducted on ten exchanges, of which the Chicago Board of Trade is the largest. You can buy or sell corn, wheat, soybeans, sugar, and pork bellies; gold, silver, platinum, foreign currencies, even Treasury bills. No matter what the commodity, all trades work in roughly the same way: If you buy a contract, you agree to accept delivery of a specified amount of the commodity at a fixed future date; if you sell a contract, you agree to deliver a specified amount of the commodity at some fixed future date. Unless you are Armour Meat or General Foods or Betty Crocker, you never expect to deliver or to take delivery of 40,000 pounds of live beef or 112,000 pounds of sugar or 5,000 bushels of wheat (each of those numbers represents one contract). Rather, if you buy a contract, you expect the price to go up. And at a certain point, before the settlement day, you will sell that contract at a profit. Similarly, if you sell a contract, you expect the price to fall. At some point in the future, again before the settlement date, you will buy a contract—hopefully, at a lower price—and close out your position.

Unlike such securities as stocks and bonds which can be put away in vaults and remembered later, an open commodities contract is not something you want to go off on a vacation and forget about. Many a weary traveler has returned home, bleary with jet lag, suitcase contents disheveled by sadistic customs inspectors, only to find 200,000 pounds of onions dumped on the front lawn. It really does happen.

Commodity trading has two major attractions: very small margin requirements (usually 5 percent and rarely more than 10 percent—compared to 50 percent for common stocks, and not all stocks are marginable) and action. Commodities is the fastest game in town. While the stock market may only drift along, pork bellies may go from 53 cents a pound to 45 cents, up to 60 cents, and back down to 53 cents, all in six months' time. Considering the size of the margin, those are big moves. You have to have the stomach to ride that kind of roller coaster.

Let me spell out my biases up front. I believe that in a free society people should be allowed to do almost anything they wish with their own money. But just as we protect minors and those we consider not capable of judgment, we should protect the individual investor to the extent that it is clear that he fully understands what he is doing and the risks he may be taking.

Wall Street makes a lot of money on commodity commissions. In times of slow stock markets in particular, those commissions may represent a sizable portion of its income. The stock market has been slow in the last few years, and I wonder how careful the Street has been to explain the risks of commodities trading to all those eager clients lining up to make that one big killing. Some firms, like Cargill Investor Services, require a minimum deposit of $10,000 from clients who will run their own accounts. That $10,000 minimum was instituted in order to shock prospective clients into the realization that playing in commodities can become bloody. But Merrill Lynch, the country's largest commodity broker, takes any account with a $2,500 minimum.

Just as options trading was hauled out of the closet to become the fastest-growing game in town, no dinner party today fails to number among its guests someone who has suddenly discovered the excitement of commodities trading. The lure of a game that can be played for five cents on the dollar is naturally irresistible to many. For others it becomes a kind of people's capitalism. Low margin requirements brought everyone into the stock market back in the 1920s. Those low margin requirements caused most people to be wiped out in the crash of 1929, as brokers began selling out their clients' accounts when the market turned down. Then, too late for many people, the Federal Reserve Board stepped in to regulate margin requirements, in effect trying to protect the individual from his own folly and naiveté. Because it is assumed that only sophisticated speculators—those who fully understand the risks and are willing to accept them—play the commodities futures game, there is thought to be no need for similar regulation of the commodities market. Yet commodities are now being hustled to almost everyone, and that's where I start blinking in disbelief.

Considering how many brokers a firm such as Merrill Lynch employs, and how few people in this country really understand the commodities markets, I wonder whether—even with the best intentions on the part of brokers—many customers really know what's going on.

What's going on is simple. Look at the study made by Blair Stewart for the Commodity Exchange Authority way back in 1949. A group of 8,782 speculators in grains were analyzed: 2,184 showed profits totaling $2,064,800, and 6,598 showed losses totaling $11,958,200. A more recent study, conducted by Thomas A. Hieronymus for the Commodity Research Bureau, examined the records for one brokerage firm in 1969: 164 accounts showed profits of $462,413, and 298 accounts showed losses of $1,127,355. Commissions paid to the broker totaled $406,344. The commissions nearly equaled total trading profits! Not bad, boys.

Commodity futures trading dates back to the early 1600s in Japan. Not surprisingly, most business was done in rice. Then, as now, major users of commodities, the trade buyers, wanted to be able to asure themselves of sufficient quantities of their raw material in the future and, if possible, to guard against severe unexpected price fluctuations. Hershey, for example, is in the business of making chocolate; it needs cocoa today, next month, and next year. It's convenient for Hershey to know today that cocoa is coming; it's also convenient to know now what cocoa will cost a year from now so that it may plan its pricing in advance. Enter the speculator. The speculator is the public.

The speculator in commodity futures takes upon himself the risks of price fluctuation. That's what Mike was doing. He thought he was working on a reliable tip, a tip that Russian buying would so increase the demand for a product whose supply was fixed (at least for the moment) that the price of the product would go up. Since this was Hollywood fantasyland, the tip turned out to be correct. In reality, however, it's not usually some big new buyer that distorts the market and causes price changes. Usually it's the weather. Too much rain in Brazil, and coffee won't grow. We all saw the effects of that a few years back when a pound of Maxwell House in the supermarket nudged $5. Or too little rain in Iowa, and the corn crop fails. A shortage of corn makes feeding pigs expensive, so farmers slaughter more, glutting the bacon market and sending prices down.

When the next cocoa fungus will hit the Ivory Coast or a new boll weevil will attack cotton is anybody's guess. And that's just what the speculator does: he guesses. To be sure, when he guesses wrong he can cut his losses, and when he's right he can pyramid his winnings. But to my mind it's still just guessing. And according to the studies, the speculator guesses wrong about 75 percent of the time.

Of course, those guesses do serve a social good: the speculator's presence in the market tends to mitigate price swings, and that may eventually be to the benefit of the ultimate consumer of chocolate bars. But I doubt that altruism is what brings speculators into the market. On that point, a recently revised book that claims to be the *ne plus ultra* of commodities dealing takes the trouble to differentiate between gambling and speculating.* Gambling, the authors say, is the creation of risk solely for the purpose of taking it in return for the opportunity to win money (as in betting on horses, poker, roulette). Speculation, however, "deals in risks that are present in the process of marketing goods in a free capitalistic system. . . . If the speculator were unwilling to take them someone else would have to do so."

There it is; if you lose money in commodities, you don't have to feel as bad as if you lost money at the track. You helped to create a social good.

We could cite people who gamble on stocks. They are usually the people who put up their money because Jenny at the canasta club said that Philip the gas station owner got a tip from Herbie the luncheonette owner who spoke to his nephew the

---

* Richard J. Tewles, et al., *The Commodity Futures Game*, New York: McGraw-Hill, 1977, pp. 4–5.

dentist who said that this little company in Peoria was about to sell seltzer to China. There are also those people, including senators before the television cameras, who hang the *Wall Street Journal* on a blackboard and throw darts. Whatever stock they hit, they buy.

If either of these methods of stock selection (or some variation thereon) is your style, commodities trading is for you. And the commodities broker would be correct in saying that his specialty is no more risky than the games you're now playing. But proper stock selection and a fair understanding of market timing can result in minimizing risks and providing rewards to prudent investors. Commodities trading is *always* a gamble. Price movements in wheat and soybeans are a function of forces beyond human control; they follow no historical pattern. With General Motors, however, we know how many cars were sold last year and the year before, and we can make a realistic approximation of what may be expected to happen next year. We can also examine how the stock price has moved and judge by price-earnings ratios whether the stock is expensive or cheap. If one gave any time at all to the process, it didn't take much to understand that General Motors stock was expensive at $85 a share and, despite a supposed oil crisis in 1975, cheap at $29 a share. You have no such opportunity with commodities. Just look at the accompanying chart of the price movements in pork bellies, and remember that because of extremely low margin requirements a movement of a few pennies in either direction (depending on which side you're on) can wipe you out. As a child I loved roller coasters, but they cost me only a dime a ride.

There's a third group playing the commodities game, along with the trade buyers and the speculators. That group is the locals, the professional commodities traders. They are the guys on the floor of the exchanges who execute orders for other brokers and also trade their own accounts. From what I've seen, the professional commodities trader has a hard time falling asleep at night, knowing that he too has no idea what tomorrow may bring—too many piglets or too few?

PORK BELLIES

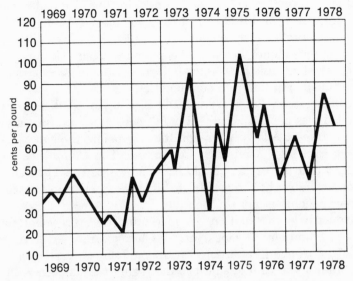

Prepared by Commodity Research Bureau, Inc., N.Y.C. 10001

Professional commodities traders take a lot of Valium. (They have also been known to rig markets. More on that later.) God only knows what the average Dick and Jane must need. The Commodity Futures Trading Commission, the federal regulatory agency for commodities trading, is trying to work up a system whereby brokers would be required to turn away or at least discourage prospective clients who are not financially or psychologically suited to the commodities game. I don't mean to sound cynical, but while I can contemplate (albeit with trepidation) the possibility of concocting some objective measure of financial suitability, I wonder how a commodities broker, who in another life may have been a shoe salesman, can be expected to be the equivalent of a trained psychoanalyst capable of understanding the complex workings of a customer's "I want to get rich" mind. May we expect brokers to equip their offices with couches for one-on-one analysis? Or gym mats for group encounter sessions?

They had better do something: Recently a twenty-one-year-old lost his mother and gained a small fortune. He had never bought a stock in his life. He had never played commodities. He met a broker and explained that he had lived well without his mother's money before and could do so again. He couldn't care less about risk. He wanted to turn his bundle into a bushel. The broker put him into commodities.

Quicker than Peter Piper could pick his pickled peppers, the kid was pecked clean. He didn't care much but his sister was outraged. A lawyer brought the case before the New York Stock Exchange Arbitration Committee. The Committee adjudged that the broker should have known better. The major brokerage firm had to reimburse all losses. Score one for Wall Street becoming more responsible.

Nevertheless, Neil J. Aslin, marketing vice president for ContiCommunity Services, Inc., of Chicago, summed it up in a 1978 *Business Week* article: "You should stay away from commodities if you cannot adjust to the reality that nobody really knows what's going to happen." A commodities broker friend of mine (who feels no need to be identified) went still further in setting out guidelines. After talking a bit about corn (the broker's best friend in commodities, for it never goes up much, never goes down much, the investor usually loses—but not much—and the broker gets all those commissions—very much indeed) he went down his list:

1. Successful commodities speculators always diversify so that wrong guesses in one commodity can be made up with right guesses in others. The typical speculator may have one or two positions at a time; the pro has as many as eighteen or twenty open positions at once. Rough translation: Don't put all your eggs or wheat or sugar in one basket.

2. Never listen to brokers. By the time they get their information from the afternoon sales meetings, it's already old news. The locals have long since received and acted upon it. By the time it's passed on to you, it's as stale as a leftover corn muffin.

3. Don't trade too much. The average guy pays his broker

full commissions that usually run somewhere between 25 percent and 50 percent of the *total equity* in the account.

4. Cut your losses. There's an old Eastern European saying that certain things are as helpful as medicine for a dead man. It's always been a waste of time to tell individuals to admit their mistakes and cut their losses. The pros do it all the time, but individuals can't seem to untangle their egos from their investments. How often have you heard (or said), "I'll just hold till I'm even, then I'll get out." And how often has the speaker gotten even?

5. If you must play in commodities and you can't afford the time to become an expert yourself, find a good fund with a proven record and join it. And that gives rise to two new concerns. First, you must make sure that the record you are given is checked out, by you or your lawyer. Ask for references and then call them. Don't believe any beautifully computerized sheets you are handed; computers print out what man puts in. Second, most of the good funds open their books to new members only once a year. You may have to be patient. A good fund will bring your commission rate down to about 8 percent. It will also usually take a piece of the profits, but more often than not there will be profits.

6. Now here's my friend's final guideline—the one guaranteed to set his colleagues on their ears: No one should play in commodities without a minimum investment of $100,000. That's right, $100,000—the minimum today that will allow you to diversify adequately and to absorb your losses without being wiped out, the minimum that will allow you to stay alive in bad times so that you can prosper in good times.

Remember, the above list isn't mine. It comes from a guy whose living depends on individuals playing in commodities. Why did he give it? He knows no one will listen! He knows commodity addicts will lose their shirts. They may be able to quit smoking, drinking, snorting, or even visiting OTB, but when it comes to "investing" in commodities, it's a different story. "My broker told me that this time summer wheat . . . ."

Of course there are exceptions. You've heard about the guy

who made a bundle. I've heard about him too.

Jerry worked for the post office. He had majored in math at college, he knew a lot about computers, and he went to the post office to reorganize systems and create greater efficiency. Jerry was a real-life Mike. A nice guy who deserved a break. As luck would have it, Jerry became fascinated with commodities in 1973, the first year in many that there was big money to be made in commodities.

Jerry found a broker but made all his own decisions. With an initial stake of $5,000, he plunged into currency futures and watched his money grow. In short order he transferred into sugar and quadrupled his money. Then he quadrupled in soybeans and tripled in copper. By 1975 his $5,000 had grown to $700,000. Along the way he had learned about silver tax straddles as a way to avoid paying taxes on his profits (see Chapter 7).

From October 1975 to March 1976 almost everyone lost in commodities. The markets moved very little in either direction. Even when you were right, the commissions ate up your profits. So Jerry gave back some, but not much.

Then came the Brazilian coffee freeze, and Jerry was off and running again. He hit the big move in soybeans in November 1976, and he counted his money: $990,000. Almost the magic number, almost a millionaire. Now he could begin to change his lifestyle. He quit the post office to devote full time to commodities. He bought a Mercedes, two New York apartments, and a house in Montauk—all mortgaged to provide maximum cash for investment. Jerry felt that 1977 was going to be his year.

You don't reach a million by accident. Jerry began to think he knew something. He forgot Socrates' warning about knowing what you don't know. Jerry took four positions in 1977: he went long coffee, soybeans, sugar, and cotton. Each went down. Jerry was dumbfounded. This couldn't be happening to him, not Jerry the millionaire, former member of the United States Postal Service. Jerry had never suffered losses before. Jerry had never learned to cut his losses. Instead he watched the house on Montauk float away, the car drive off, and the bank collect the two apartments.

Jerry still has $9,000. And once again he is on salary at the post office. All in all, it didn't work out too badly. His first million began with a $5,000 bankroll; maybe the $9,000 will grow to $2 million. Maybe the nice guy will win after all.

Perhaps the worst thing to happen to the investor, vis-à-vis commodities, was the introduction of contracts for Treasury bills, Fannie Maes (Federal National Mortgage Association bonds), and other financial instruments. In the hands of the ultrasophisticated, these new contracts can be valuable additions to the money manager's pool of resources. Many banks are using Treasury bill futures as a hedge to protect income from investment portfolios. If interest rates go down, for example, losses on the portfolio would be made up on the gains of the futures contracts; if interest rates go up, the converse would be true. In either case, the portfolio could be arranged to maintain a predetermined level of income. Thus banks and pension funds have become hedges in their fields just as General Mills and others are hedgers, not speculators, in theirs.

However, most investors are not sophisticated bank trust managers. Naive investors may begin to think that what's good for the pro must be good for them, too. And into commodities they plunge—invariably, not as hedgers but as speculators.

As one might expect, the massive growth of commodities trading has brought with it a flow of charges that prices are being rigged by insiders in a number of commodities, particularly potatoes and soybeans. The Commodity Futures Trading Commission will be there looking for industry problems, but it won't be easy to discover them. In 1978, 43 million futures contracts worth more than $1.5 trillion were traded in 37 different commodities on ten exchanges; the total should grow to $2 trillion in 1979, up 33.3 percent. The commissioner will have his hands full looking for needles in all those haystacks.

One of the great problems with the commodities market, and one of the great unseen dangers for outside speculators (let's drop the pretense of calling them investors) is that prices are relatively easy to rig. There are safeguards against such rigging, but they don't usually work.

Suppose an investor buys 100 or even 1,000 shares of General Motors. If the market goes down, there will always be someone who is willing to buy that 100 or 1,000 shares of General Motors at the current market price from the unfortunate investor who guessed wrong and wants to cut his losses. But if some mutual fund had decided to buy 1 million shares of GM and the market went down, finding a buyer for that lot might be more difficult, particularly if there has been some bad news about GM.

Because the commodities markets are relatively small and each participant, however margined, is relatively large, finding buyers or sellers is not always a simple process. At any given time, in any commodity, there are speculators on both sides of the market: some who shorted contracts, expecting to cover those shorts as prices fell, and others who went long, expecting to sell those contracts as prices rose. No speculator wants to deliver or to have delivered the actual commodity. All contracts have a due date, and when that day approaches the fervor of activity increases as buyers and sellers try to close out their positions. One more factor in commodities trading is that all listed commodities have stop prices: they are permitted to rise or fall only by a given amount each day. If a commodity rises to its stop price and no one wants to sell at that price, no one buys. Trading in that commodity stops. The following day the price may open higher and go the daily limit, but again, in a rising market no one may want to sell. The process will continue day by day until the contract expiration date arrives.

Here's how rigging occurs: The locals (the floor traders) know how many wheat contracts are short. Therefore they know, particularly if prices have risen, how many speculators will be wanting to buy contracts to cover those short positions as delivery day approaches. The speculator who wants to get out early can usually do so, but human nature being what it is, many wait until the last minute, hoping that prices will fall and allow them to convert their losses to gains. Here comes the rigger.

No one individual can hold futures contracts covering more than 3 million bushels of wheat. But what if four or five large holders meet in the privacy of the men's room and decide not only to buy their limit but to hold that amount, refusing to sell until the eleventh hour to all those speculators who are trying desperately to cover their losing positions? Such collusive activity is of course strictly verboten, but you have to *prove* that it's happening. Meanwhile, the speculator can't cut his losses even if he's smart enough to try to do so. Each day the price of wheat rises to its limit, trading stops without a seller in sight, and the poor speculator is turning gently in the breeze. Prices keep rising as D-Day approaches, and no one is selling. The locals are making a killing, and the little guy's having heart failure. Finally, miraculously, the big holders all begin to sell at the same moment, to anyone who now *must* meet their inflated price. And the sad speculator must because someone out there is waiting to take delivery of the wheat the poor jerk has promised to provide.

In this example the locals, the floor brokers, were trading against their own customers. Not legal, not ethical, not nice. But what the hell? Squeezing the "shorts" goes on all the time, and when the stakes are high, cheating is called capitalism. At this writing the Commodity Futures Trading Commission is investigating the activities of Leslie Rosenthal, who with two other traders accumulated huge holdings of March wheat. In the final three days of trading the March contracts, the three held dominant positions and anyone wanting to buy had to go to them. No one has made accusations of wrongdoing, but the *New York Times* estimated that every one-cent increase in the price of March wheat meant $75,000 to the trio. The Chicago Board of Trade is the nation's largest commodities market; Leslie Rosenthal, who according to the *Times* was involved in a similar episode last December, is its vice chairman. *Beati qui ambulant in lege domini.*

To help the "investor" who is wise enough to know how little he knows about commodities, many firms have devised "guided" or "managed" commodity accounts. No one knows

for sure, but there is probably more than $150 million worth
of those accounts in the Street these days, some of them advertised as a logical alternative for those who are disappointed
with current rates of return on stocks, bonds, and savings accounts. One firm, Fairchild, Arabatzis & Smith, advertised in
the *New York Times* help-wanted columns for registered commodities salespeople, announcing "a dynamic new concept in
managed accounts where the highly volatile commodities market is tracked daily by computer and our skilled professional
traders are there to advise and supervise all trading . . . usher-
ing in a new era in commodity marketing."

They did usher in a new era in commodity marketing. In
February 1979, in a case prosecuted by the United States Attorney's office in the Southern District of New York, Fairchild,
Arabatzis & Smith was shut down and Steven M. Arabatzis
pleaded guilty to charges of defrauding customers of about
$6 million, mainly through the sale of contracts for the deferred
delivery of gold.

This particular game is played under many names: forward
delivery contracts, deferred delivery contracts, limited risk for-
wards. Victims are suckered in with the offer of risk-free opportunities to hedge against inflation and (at the same time) to
cash in on rising gold or silver prices. Many investors have
put up large sums of money, usually tens of thousands of dollars,
to reserve the opportunity to buy gold or other commodities
at a fixed price in the future. They weren't buying contracts,
they were only reserving opportunities. They were buying
options on commodity futures while thinking they were paying
for the gold itself.

Unlike options on common stocks, it is illegal to sell commodity options in the United States. But the commodity business
is still a largely unregulated business, and recent disclosures
have shown that the crooked entrepreneur has lots of room
to work in. So far firms such as Fairchild, Arabatzis & Smith
are not required to register with anyone. By the time the Commodity Futures Trading Commission receives complaints,
many boiler rooms will have closed up shop and moved on.

On February 25, 1979, the *New York Times* reported the plight of one Albert M. Lincoln, a forty-two-year-old California businessman. Lincoln received three telephone calls from an employee of First National Bullion Corporation in New York (since closed down by the authorities), offering to sell him three-month or six-month contracts for gold futures. The caller predicted that the price of gold would reach $350 an ounce by March 1979.

Lincoln was told that he could buy a contract for 100 ounces of gold with an effective price of $214.50 an ounce (that day's price) and that when the contract came due in six months he would have three alternatives: to buy the gold at $214.50, even if the price were then higher; to liquidate his position and collect the profits if the price were higher; or to purchase gold at the then market price if gold should, unexpectedly, be below the $214.50 price. For only $6,800 he could lock in a position for each 100-ounce contract. Sounded good to Lincoln; he made three payments totaling $33,500. It was not until several months later that he discovered that the payments were nonrefundable fees that would not be applied to his ultimate purchases. Then the firm closed up.

Translation: Lincoln was sold (illegally) options to buy gold futures. If within the six-month period gold rose from $214.50 to $281.50, he would break even. At any price at or below $214.50 he could buy all the gold he wanted, just as anyone else could. But his options would be worthless, and he would be (and he was) out $33,500.

Get-rich-quick schemes have worked for years, and they are probably working on other Albert Lincolns today. It's one thing to get yourself in trouble by not knowing what you're doing but at least doing it with a reputable firm. However, to answer the ads or the telephone calls of unknowns and to send them money defies all sense and logic.

Still it goes on. Consider this, from the promotional literature of the firm of J. M. King & Associates: "The word is beginning to get out: the middle-income investor can also make money in the commodities markets just as the insiders do. If he has the right kind of expert advice. . . . the only way most non-professional investors can gain access to this kind of inside information is through a team of professional money managers working literally around the clock. J. M. King & Associates, like most successful futures traders, operates with the benefit of detailed information provided by a platoon of computers and a network of expert brokers roaming the floors of various exchanges. . . ."

Not a single illegal word in this promotion. And no warnings. No mention of the one winner for every five losers. How easy for the unsophisticated to fall for this kind of hype! And as yet there's no Ralph Nader to fight to protect the lambs who are being led to slaughter in this barely regulated industry.

Most managed account programs—the legitimate ones—charge only a commission for trades. Some, however, run by outside "advisers," often charge management fees of about 6 percent of equity and take an average of 10 to 15 percent of the profits. But the average managed account, even at a first-rate firm, might spend 15 to 25 percent of its equity on commissions alone, and aggressive action in volatile markets has been known to run up commission charges of 50 percent, 100 percent, even 200 percent of the initial equity outlay. If they make you a bundle, there's nothing to complain about. But considering the frequency of profits, it sure sounds like churning to me.

Managed accounts are unquestionably the next big trouble area for an industry that already has enough trouble to keep it busy for a long time to come. If you must deal in commodities, then, understand that they're not an alternative to past mistakes in the stock market; understand that the streets are paved with pavement and that only the other guy ever gets rich quick. If you must gamble, do it with that 5 percent or 10 percent or whatever part of your portfolio you can afford to lose—in commodities the odds are five to one you will.

2 + 2 = 5 (SOMETIMES)

Tax shelter: 1: a method by which an individual minimizes payments due to a government. 2: same as 1, but easily overlooked by those prone to masochistic surrender (see *sour grapes*). 3: (obsolete?) a device by which a fool and his money are easily parted (see *shell game*).

To varying degrees tax shelters fit each of the above definitions. To the layman, when he thinks of them at all, tax shelters evoke images of back-room politicians and shady businessmen bilking the upstanding middle classes by not carrying their fair share of the tax burden. One thinks of extravagant corporate boardrooms and batteries of high-priced lawyers and accountants searching for any scheme or loophole that will allow their already too powerful clients to become still richer by wringing from the tax system the last drop of personal advantage.

These perceptions have often been valid. The press and other media have been filled with stories of cattle ranches and breeding farms, oil explorations and real estate deals designed not to make money but to avoid the taxation of the very rich. We shudder when politicians who run for office reveal income tax data that show years of six-figure incomes balanced by tax payments that are smaller than those of factory assembly line workers. One can only speculate whether Ronald Reagan lost the 1976 Republican presidential nomination to Gerald Ford because of their ideological differences or because Reagan's tax returns, after grudgingly being given to the press, revealed that he was so well sheltered that for many years he had avoided payment of any substantial federal taxes.

Tax shelters don't deserve their bad press. They are usually investments through which individuals legitimately reduce or defer tax payments to the Government. They include the special treatment of capital gains, whereby profits on investments held for a specific length of time are taxed at a lower rate than ordinary income; the interest received on municipal bonds, which is wholly exempt from federal taxes; the interest on certain United States government obligations, which is exempt from city and state taxation; the investment tax credit, whereby a portion of one's tax obligation is offset by new investment in plant and equipment; and rapid depreciation, which allows an investment in capital goods to be written off more quickly than might economically be required. In each of these cases, tax shelters were created to induce individuals to divert portions of their incomes to areas considered worthy of special treatment by those who write the tax laws. In the case of capital gains, it encourages new investment in the American economy. Lending to municipal governments allows municipalities to borrow at lower rates than their corporate counterparts, ostensibly to use those borrowings for nonprofit, socially relevant projects. And both the investment tax credit and rapid depreciation encourage the formation of new capital goods. Each of these types of investment reduces the taxpayer's current income tax bill.

Almost everyone uses tax shelters to defer the payment of income taxes. Under the law, certain portions of current income may be diverted to funds that accumulate for an individual's retirement years. While we do not pay any taxes on those monies now, we will be taxed at ordinary income tax rates when we begin drawing on them. Since it is assumed that our incomes after retirement will be lower than they are during our "productive" years, retirement incomes will fall into a lower tax bracket. All pension plans, Keogh funds, and Individual Retirement Accounts (IRAs) fit into this category, as do certain forms of trust accounts set up for children or heirs.

Aside from periodic attempts by Congress to raise or lower the taxes on capital gains, none of these areas has received much attention. They are universally accepted as the legitimate prerogatives of a free economic system in which, at least in part, individuals retain a right and a responsibility to care for themselves and their society.

Why then have other tax shelters aroused so much controversy? Because they have been used by clever tax planners in a manner that observes the letter of the law but destroys its intent. Let's look at an example.

Suppose you were to buy a building as a rental investment. You might put up 30 percent of the $100,000 cost and borrow the rest from a bank at 9 percent interest. At the end of the year (for tax purposes) you have an interest expense of $6,300. If the $30,000 you invested came from current income, you would pay income taxes on $30,000 less $6,300 in deductible expenses. In addition, you could depreciate the value of the building over its expected life of twenty years. This would give you an additional expense for tax purposes of $5,000. Thus the government would expect you to pay taxes on income of $18,700 ($30,000 less total expenses of $11,300). All perfectly legitimate; this hardly fits into the category of tax shelter.

Now let's look at a slightly different example. Suppose you and a group of similar investors were to buy a shopping complex. A bank is now lending to a big business enterprise. It may be willing to lend 95 percent of the cost of the project. In some cases the bank may demand personal guarantees in the event the future value of the investment should not be able to cover the full amount of the loan. In most cases, however, the loan will be made without recourse to the investor. In a nonrecourse investment, if you put up 5 percent and borrow the rest of your share, a $30,000 investment would allow a borrowing of $570,000. (At 9 percent the interest would come to $51,300.) So far, on an investment of $30,000, the taxpayer has an offsetting expense of $51,300. Not bad.

It gets even better. If one chooses to depreciate the project rapidly, perhaps over ten years rather than twenty, the depreciation deduction on your portion of the investment amounts to another $60,000 (one-tenth of $600,000). Thus your investment of only $30,000 has brought you, in the first of many years, an offsetting deduction of $111,300 ($51,300 plus $60,000), which can be applied to all other ordinary income you had that year. Of course, when you receive rents from your investment property, you will pay ordinary income taxes on them. But that will be later, and most of us live for today. Moreover, should the complex be sold at a future date (this would usually be planned for ten years hence, when the depreciation allowance runs out), any profit on the sale will be taxed only at the special capital gains rates.

All this was once legal, but it wasn't exactly what the congressional tax planners had had in mind. Consequently the Tax Reform Act of 1978 put an end to nonrecourse tax exemptions. Today exemptions for tax purposes (exclusive of investment tax credits) can be claimed only to an amount equal to the actual amount of money an investor has at risk.

It was fun while it lasted. But now that tax shelters have become more limited, an investor must be even more careful about the proliferating schemes that are being placed before him.

Let's go back to the beginning, and the beginning is April 15, any April 15. When we work out our tax returns, we can do one of three things: (1) We can pay exactly the amount due the government, but that is rather hard to do. So much of the tax law is vague and subject to individual interpretation that it would be virtually impossible for two accountants, or even two Internal Revenue Service examiners, to agree on all items to the last dollar. (2) We could consciously underpay. But then we would risk going to jail. (3) We could overpay our taxes. Idiotic! Yet that is exactly what most of us do each year. We overpay, sometimes out of timidity, because we fear being audited. (It has been suggested, usually by our less than efficient accountants, that being called for an audit is a shame that falls somewhere between being named corespondent in a divorce proceeding and being caught shoplifting.) Or we overpay from lack of knowledge as to what items may be legitimately deducted.

If we add our figures incorrectly, even to the advantage of the government, efficient computers will announce that we have made a mistake. The government is very honest that way. But if we simply neglect certain deductions or fail to arrange our financial lives in such a way as to allow the existence of those deductions, the government does not come back to us offering a basic course in tax planning. Rather, the government assumes that we care enough about money to know what we are doing with it. Some of us do. Most of us only think we do.

Whether we prepare our tax returns ourselves or have accountants do them for us, we try to take whatever deductions are legitimately due us. Would anyone not claim the $750 personal exemption? Not claim medical expenses, charitable donations, or professional books or journals? Or the price of this book? The tax forms that we receive each year boldly state that, if married, we should first work out individual returns, then joint returns, and finally submit whichever results in a lower tax bill.

If we use accountants, we pay their tax-deductible fee not for their filling in numbers for us and neatly typing and photocopying our returns but rather for their professional expertise, which will enable us to pay a lower tax than we would have paid had we done the work ourselves. Certainly there is nothing immoral in that. (Unless, of course, by using accountants we pay more than we would have paid had we done the work ourselves—but that is a different dimension of immorality.)

Today it is illegal to deduct the cost of a child's private school education. Should the law be changed, however, would anyone in such a situation not claim the deduction? Only if he did not know about it. And that is what our accountants are for. It is for them to know. But what if we neglected to tell them that we have a child attending private school? Worse, what if they neglected to ask? That, in a nutshell, is most people's problem with tax shelters: they know not what to tell, and too often they are being serviced by accountants who neglect to ask. Thus the individual, logically but erroneously, concludes that the tax laws must have been written for the special few and not for him.

No accountant can be efficient when he does not know his client's entire history. He is then constrained to work within the limits his clients impose through their silence. It is incumbent upon us to insist on having the time to educate our accountants. Unless we use H. & R. Block, we are already paying for the time that such education takes. But often we must know to take the initiative, and even then, we have to make sure that we are educating the right person. Accountants and lawyers, like doctors, have become specialized. Even in the largest firms only one or perhaps two partners are experts in tax planning. The others would probably stare blankly at us if we suddenly wondered out loud which tax shelters, if any, suited our individual financial situation. At that point one could test the worth of an accountant: If the blank stare yielded a questioning call to someone who could help, we are probably on the road to getting our money's worth; if, however, it resulted only in an awkward change of subject, the road to one's money's worth begins at the nearest door.

What I have said so far is not at all exaggerated. If anything is exaggerated, it is the reliance we place on people who have titles. Dr. Foreman was one such person; he trusted his accountant. But his story has a happy ending.

Dr. Foreman is a well-known psychoanalyst with a well-deserved reputation. Dr. Foreman also knows a lot about art. But Dr. Foreman doesn't know very much about money. So he retained an accountant—a very solicitous one (and a very expensive one).

Dr. Foreman isn't exactly poor. About twenty years ago he inherited a stock portfolio that was then valued at $400,000. It is still worth $400,000. He could have done better in a savings account, yet he has still done better than most. Art, however, has made him rich. He has no training and a perfect eye. He can spot talent before anyone else, and whomever he has spotted others have come to admire and to pay for. Starting many years ago with just a few hundred dollars, Dr. Foreman kept trading up and now has a collection that sports such names as Picasso, Klee, and Moore.

Recently he decided to buy an apartment. He knew he could afford the $90,000 price, but he didn't know the best way to raise the money. So he consulted his accountant. The response was direct, definitive, and absolute: Sell the Picasso.

I come into the story at the farewell dinner party—a farewell to the orgiastic fusion celebrated on canvas. It would be off the next day to the gallery for sale. I ruined the party.

When I discovered why we had come together, I took the good doctor aside. We talked about the facts of life, but this time the analyst was on the couch.

The painting had a cost value of $42,000. Its market value was $187,000. If the painting were sold, Dr. Foreman would have to pay a capital gains tax of 35 percent on the difference: 35 percent of $145,000, or $50,750 to the government. Dr. Foreman isn't stupid, but no one had bothered to tell him that he had alternatives. One was to sell stock. Since his portfolio had not appreciated, no tax would be due—a quick saving of $50,750! Better still, Dr. Foreman could borrow from a bank against his securities. The dividends on his stocks would cover the interest payments, and the possibility that his stocks would increase in value (this was 1977, when most securities were underpriced) would be retained.

As for the accountant, I can't presume to know what he had been thinking. Whatever it was, Dr. Foreman no longer cares.

Contrary to popular opinion, most tax shelters were introduced to this country by the Congress of the United States. In an act that it has not really regretted, the government recognized that intelligent entrepreneurs, if allowed to retain some portion of their income that would otherwise flow into the United States Treasury, might better be able to use those monies for investment in areas that would ultimately prove more advantageous to the country's economic well-being than if the government collected and spent them.

What the tax writers did not understand was the conflicting morality that has always been rampant in America. There are people who are willing and able to drive Mack trucks through any small loophole in the tax law. To them true capitalist morality is reflected in the lowest possible payment of taxes. Let the government worry about the spirit of the law; they will stick to its letter. Because of the excesses of these people, tax shelters have, in part, received the bad press they continue to enjoy.

The rest of the tax shelters' notoriety comes through fraud, and this brings us to the other side of the moral conflict. Hundreds of thousands of Americans could and should shelter some of their incomes. But to do so strikes them as immoral and slightly dirty. Given the choice between paying additional taxes and feeling underhanded, they will of course opt for lower taxes and go to psychiatrists to work off their guilt and their seemingly excessive after-tax incomes. Unfortunately, their guilt prevents them from being as inquisitive or as analytical as they should be about those monies destined for tax shelters. They don't want to know much about them—just let the deed be done, and don't tarnish them with details. What an opening for that other kind of American entrepreneur, commonly known as the wolf in sheep's clothing, the hustler, the crook. More about him later. But first, the innovative tax avoider.

Not long ago I lunched with a friend at the Club, that private watering hole for Wall Streeters perched atop the World Trade Center. Any evening and all day on weekends the public may use the same premises (its name then is Windows on the World), but Monday through Friday at lunch only members enjoy Warren Platner's $8 million modern evocation of Versailles. Now my friend is a corporate finance man, one of the best. He has helped major companies merge and spin off. He knows everything there is to know about tax-loss carry-forwards and stock buyouts. He can put together a proxy fight with the best of them, and he can demonstrate to a recalcitrant owner a thousand reasons why his company should be sold to the local conglomerate. My friend lives with his wife and two children in a neat house on the other side of the George Washington Bridge and summers unostentatiously in an unchic mountain area near Lake George. Both homes were furnished with the aid of a not particularly inspired sister-in-law cum interior decorator. The Bloomingdale's touch is evident, along with art of the Greenwich Village summer street show variety—colorful but of a quality one notch below his five-year-old's finger painting.

We examined the view, made our pro forma comments on the Statue of Liberty and the current state of the stock market, and then the conversation turned to art. Art from my friend? I hadn't thought he had set foot in a museum since his mother signed the pass allowing him to accompany his seventh-grade class on a bus trip to see the mummies. And here he was talking of modern art. Not, to be sure, about its aesthetic value, but about present and future price expectations. He told me that one particular artist, not quite the darling of the nouvelle vague set, was soon to become the highest-priced living American artist. Now, I'd consider selling my every possession if this Wall Street mavin told me to put my money into Martian Widgets Corporation. But art?

He thought I might be interested in a sale that would take place two weeks hence at Parke Bernet. Some of his artist's lithographs would be auctioned, along with some works of other artists whose names he couldn't remember—like Matisse and Braque.

I saw him at the auction. You couldn't miss him; he resembled no one else in the Madison Avenue crowd. The auction was largely uneventful, almost boring in its predictability. Then came his artist. The bidding began as any other. But it didn't stop. Two bidders, at opposite sides of the room, continued after all others had dropped out. Neither would relent. The price went higher and higher. People stopped whispering to one another about the next item and watched with rapt attention. Eyes moved from bidder to bidder. When it was over, one lithograph had sold for $84,000—a world record.

It turned out that my friend had gotten together a small syndicate. Quietly they had bought a portfolio of the artist's lithographs, one hundred in all, for roughly $100,000. Then they had arranged for two friends to bid against each other at the next public auction. The $84,000 price had instantly jumped the "market value" of the syndicate's portfolio from $100,000 to $8.4 million. Not that anyone could be found to pay that price; but they could donate the portfolio to a museum. And donate they did, an $8.4 million gift—and, coincidentally, an $8.4 million tax write-off.

The Internal Revenue Service didn't like the deal very much. But there's no accounting for taste. And the last price paid determines value. My friend was an artful dodger if ever there was one.

The problem with the deal thought up by my friend, and others like it, is that they can cause trouble for the rest of us. Sure, it conformed to the letter of the law even if the spirit was somewhat transgressed. But it also alerted the IRS, and the IRS may just be a bit more quizzical the next time we try to donate Grandma's patchwork quilt to a charity bazaar, or that seven-foot birdcage made entirely of Good Humor sticks to the Museum of Primitive Art.

Eventually, in its infinite wisdom and with what has come to be known as deliberate speed, the government does get around to closing the loopholes in our tax system that many of my Wall Street acquaintances see as treasures waiting to be hunted. Recently the *Wall Street Journal* reported one such closure. It concerned commodity straddles, and the anguished wail of commodity specialists, who for years had been reaping small fortunes from this one, can still be heard. It went this way:

For his fee, the commodity specialist arranged for customers a complicated series of transactions known as tax straddle butterfly spreads. They involved a variety of simultaneous positions on both the buy and sell sides of the silver futures market. The positions would be unwound in each of two different tax years, intentionally creating a short-term loss in the current year that was matched exactly to a long-term capital gain in the next. Thus, because of the special tax treatment of capital gains, the short-term (ordinary) tax loss generated a lower tax bill than that which would be paid in the following year at the much lower long-term capital gains tax rate.

The maneuver did not need to end there. What works for one set of years can work for others, and the sophisticated would continually roll over their positions. Every year, like magic, tax losses (not real losses, mind you) would suddenly appear. The alchemists were on the right track after all: there is a way to turn baser metal into gold. A $10,000 loss matched by a $10,000 gain was not, as any simple-minded person would surmise, a wash. It was a paper tax loss that could be applied against any other ordinary income derived during the tax period. And the boys in this ball park weren't exactly going hungry.

Don't be surprised if you haven't heard much about this little number. Although firms like Merrill Lynch, E. F. Hutton, and Loeb Rhoades were creating losses by the billions for their customers (and not doing so badly for themselves on the commissions generated), they kept it pretty quiet. There were no big television spots to proclaim that Merrill Lynch was bullish on tax dodges. In fact, when the head of Merrill's tax straddle department wanted to write customers to tell them of this delectable, surefire service, counsel advised that such a letter might bring this area to the attention of the Internal Revenue Service, which then might try to put an end to the party. Well, somehow the IRS got wind of it anyway—about ten years after everyone else. Not only did the IRS say cease and desist, but in a very unsportsmanlike manner it had the audacity to make its ruling retroactive for three years. IRS Ruling 77-185 is being appealed by some of this country's biggest legal guns. It's not fair, they say, to take away such nice games.

As far as I can tell, the single most compelling legal argument for the preservation of tax straddles is that they were used for so long without anyone bothering anybody.

For those of you who might have wanted to play this game, all is not lost. The IRS still has to prove that each transaction was deliberately entered into only for the purpose of achieving a tax loss. After all, sometimes these losses do occur because an investor played silver wrong. It could have gone up when it should have gone down. The legal fees should cost the IRS—and us taxpayers, however well sheltered we may be—millions.

If these stories have made you wince a bit, let me turn quickly to the other side of the tax shelter gambit. This is the side that involves wolves and Little Red Riding Hood. Only this time Little Red loses not just her tax write-off (the worst that could have happened to our silver speculators) but everything else as well. While one side of our nature may secretly, perhaps guiltily, applaud the inventiveness of the true (now almost extinct) native capitalist who can create the really big tax fraud and get away with it, the other side of our nature demands retribution. How long can these deeds go unpunished? Well, punishment came big not too long ago, and that brings us back to the wolves.

You see, most tax shelters are relatively safe and entail little risk. But the lure of ever greater and larger tax write-offs sometimes makes the most sophisticated forget that the game is to save, not lose, money. This scheme involved tank cars, the kind that carry oil and gas across the country on 400-car-long freight trains. And the Little Red Riding Hoods were not just your everyday sophisticated investors; they included many of the partners of one of the best known and most respected Wall Street brokerage houses.

A group approached this firm seeking partners to buy $25 million worth of tank cars. The partners would enjoy large tax write-offs as the full $25 million investment was rapidly depreciated in the early years of the partnership. Later, as the rental income from the tank cars (leased to major railroads) began to flow in, the original investment of each partner would be returned. Although any profits would be taxed as ordinary income, the original tax write-offs would stand. (It should be noted that the government encourages this kind of tax shelter because it keeps railroad equipment manufacturers in business and promotes business investment and economic growth.)

The Wall Streeters liked the deal, too. The firm's partners got first crack. Clients of the firm were then introduced to the sponsors to pick up whatever crumbs were left. Each share sold for $70,000. Now, people really savvy to tax shelters know better than to use their own money. Each participant put up $10,000 and on his own credit borrowed the remaining $60,000 from the bank. Get it? The interest on the borrowed $60,000 is also tax-deductible! If one tax shelter is good, two have to be better.

Being a small, closely knit group, the sponsors wanted to do something special for the participants. Each partner was given a suitably inscribed miniature Lionel tank car, a kind of inside joke, to sit on his desk and proclaim his participation in the deal. Then the sponsors gathered up the $25 million and left for Rio. Best information has it that they are still there, enjoying the sun and the absence of an extradition treaty. Why no one bothered to check out the credentials of the sponsors, or at least to require proper custodianship of the funds, has never been made clear. What is clear is that those little tank cars were certainly the most expensive child's toy ever conceived.

What makes the train deal strange is the fact that it was not the exception that proved a rule. Cases of tax shelter fraud occur regularly, and more often than not they involve investors who one would have thought knew better. In the Home Stake Oil swindle, Oklahoma promoter Robert Simons Trippet and his corporate cohorts managed to raise $140 million, ostensibly to drill for oil, from Alan Alda, Jack Benny, Candice Bergen, Liza Minnelli, Jacob Javits, Thomas Gates (a former secretary of defense and chairman of Morgan Guaranty Trust), David Mahoney (chairman of Norton Simon, Inc.), and hundreds of highly sophisticated investors. The Home Stake bubble burst in 1974. When the air had cleared, it was determined that $30 million had been spent on drilling for oil and $110 million had disappeared (how much of that went into which foreign bank accounts is impossible to tell). An Oklahoma judge found Trippet guilty of one count of conspiracy and nine counts of mail fraud. His sentence was one day in jail; three years supervised probation; a $19,000 fine; and a $100,000 contribution to a fund for civil claimants. One may correctly infer that the presiding judge had not been a Home Stake investor.

In 1976 an equally luminous list of suckers put up $112 million for a tax shelter deal based on a nonexistent Wyoming coal mine. That case will be in the courts for years, and it is assumed that justice will again be served. It might also be assumed that at this very moment someone, somewhere, is putting together a deal to sell something that isn't anything to someone who isn't anyone. *Caveat emptor.*

Fortunately, there are decent people around who will give guidance to those smart enough to ask for it, people who will even put their own money into the investments they recommend.

Bill Noe is a peculiar kind of American capitalist. He believes in tax shelters because he believes that the individual can do better with his money than the government can do for him. He is also honest. Put together the two qualities and you have a partner in a firm that specializes in bringing together investors and thoroughly investigated business opportunities that also shelter income.

Bill began his working life carrying a degree from the B School. The Harvard Business School prides itself on teaching its students at least two things: (1) if you tell people that you went to the B School, they will know it was Harvard, and (2) any graduate of the B School is prepared to become president of any major corporation in America—indeed, in the world. Bill wanted a career in international finance.

Diploma in hand, he returned to California to look for a job. What he found was a hypochondriac father, dying from his latest imaginings and determined to spend what little was left of his life in Hawaii. The family's real estate holdings were entrusted to Bill.

He was ready. He diligently applied to the business of real estate speculation all the tools Harvard had given him: financial analysis, planning, marketing strategies, human resource development. The case method in action. Bill did everything the books had taught him. About a year later, his money gone and the lenders ready to foreclose on his properties, Bill decided to get a real job.

He found one working for Kirk Douglas, who needed someone to analyze and manage his own rather sizable real estate holdings. Bill met the movie stars and the movie people and learned a lot about real estate. But mainly he learned about tax shelters.

Hollywood soon palled, and Bill left to rebuild his fortune in the rough-and-tumble financial world of New York. Stocks and bonds, he thought; that's where the action is. He arrived in the Big Apple just after the crash of 1971. Fortunately, he knew nothing about stocks and bonds. Nobody wanted them in 1971. The pros needed new kinds of investments to sell to their clients. Considering how much the clients had lost, it's hard to believe they needed tax shelters or could afford real estate. But that's what was selling.

Bill went back into real estate. By 1973 his firm was doing $120 million a year in FHA-insured government housing—safe, legal, and a good tax shelter. But with a freeze on government-insured housing about to take effect in 1974, our hero began searching for other worthwhile real estate investments (and tax shelters) for his clients. He viewed every project he recommended, from Brundidge, Alabama, to Fond du Lac, Wisconsin. These real estate investments worked out well for Bill's clients. But the concept, with some modification, had already become the basis for one of Wall Street's most reprehensible fiascos of the 1970s, the Real Estate Investment Trust (REIT).

In 1971 Wall Street needed a new game. The stock market was in chaos and the first cutbacks were beginning in the brokerage firms. Corporations had stopped selling stocks and bonds to the public through their Wall Street intermediaries. A bat-tered public yearned for safety. Where would the revenue come from? Real estate, said Wall Street. And it's tax sheltered to boot. The Street began peddling REITs to anyone it could grab. Your money was in something solid, cemented to the ground. The real estate market boomed, as business flourished into rural America. Shares in REITs were traded on major stock exchanges. Buy, buy, buy. The word spread: you can't lose in real estate. Even the little guy caught on (or Wall Street caught him on). A new buying panic developed. We're in the money, we're in the land! Happy days were here again. Even the stock market woke up, went along with the Nixon boom, and soared to new highs.

REITs were not actually tax sheltered. In fact they were not exactly safe. Set up by the brokerage firms as trusts, the trust paid no taxes and could flow whatever income it earned directly to the investor, bypassing normal corporate taxation. Most mutual funds are organized that way. But no matter. In the early 1970s most investors believed, and were encouraged to believe, that their money was sheltered.

Usually the broker setting up the trust would raise 25 percent of the cost of a real estate project from investors. He'd take his fee off the top. Banks, which wouldn't lend money directly to developers in 1971 (developers usually needed to borrow 95 percent or more of the total project cost), were happy to lend money to the REITs because their 25 percent investment in the project cushioned the bank's exposure to loss. Some banks actually set up subsidiaries to act as consultants to REITs. One of these was Chase Mortgage Investors, a subsidiary of the Chase Manhattan Bank. CMI would borrow money from Chase and then relend that money to the REITs at higher interest rates. CMI also took a consulting fee. One wonders whether most investors thought that the Chase Manhattan Bank was behind their trusts. If they had read the fine print, they would have known better.

People weren't thinking much then about rising interest rates, double-digit inflation, or the winding down of the Vietnam War. Banks and brokers liked the bull market. It made them look good, and it made them rich. America was experiencing a new prosperity.

Then the Arabs embargoed oil and Nixon slipped on Watergate. Yet another bubble had burst. The market crashed, but those who had invested in REITs had land and buildings. Only they had overmortgaged land and unrentable buildings. The sophisticated investor should have known what he was doing and hedged his bets. The little guy had been seduced, and once again seduction turned to rape. REITs went bust, and Chase Manhattan and other banks, the original lenders, claimed the best properties. The bank could afford to wait for the market to turn. The little guy couldn't. Embarrassed, he went off to a corner and wondered if Las Vegas would have been more fun.

REITs won't go down in history as a fraudulent scheme in the class of Home Stake Oil or last year's coal scandal. After all, the buildings were usually there. But once again Wall Street had cheated the little investor, and as yet he has no good way of getting even.

The good tax-sheltered business situations still work out well for investors who clearly understand them and are able to afford whatever risks may be involved. Sometimes even some of the bad ones have had silver (or oil) linings.

In 1970 Joseph Kotler was president of Warner Broadcasting. He had a six-figure income and lived in Rye, New York. He paid his high-bracket taxes in full and thought tax shelters were for the other guy. Then Jack Warner sold his company to Kinney. Joe had a five-year contract, but now had to rethink his future. He knew he'd be in demand. But would he want to be? Perhaps it was time to try to conserve current income.

Friends had been telling him for years about the tax advantage in cattle breeding. He hadn't forgotten. Joe's a cautious man, sophisticated enough to know the fate of fools and their money. In his work he had traveled throughout the country, visiting every television station in America. He had come to know a lot of people. One was a lawyer in Traverse City, Michigan, which may be as far away from anywhere as you can get. The last time Joe had been there, the lawyer had talked about putting together cattle deals.

He renewed the contact and found that a group was being formed to buy a farm to breed Black Angus cattle. He liked the lawyer and knew that no country lawyer would dare to put one over on a big-city executive. So Joe joined the club. They bought the farm, and breeders in the area were happy to sell cows and a prize-winning bull to this sophisticated city group.

The bull alone goes for $150,000, probably twice what any yokel farmer would have paid for him. So what? Cows and bulls have twelve-year breeding lives, and the IRS says that cattle can be depreciated over a seven-year period. Depreciate a cow? Well, tax savings are tax savings.

Joe is landed gentry—at least until the phone rings in Rye. The lawyer is loath to report that someone has stolen the fornicating bull. Rustlers in the 1970s, and not a Lone Ranger in sight! Not only are the partners not going to make any money, they're out 150 grand. Joe was cowed. Years of conservatism, his first plunge, and now he's drowning. The cows are sold off, and Joe and his partners are wiped out of the cattle business. *Quod licet bovi, non licet Joe-vi.* He has learned his lesson the hard way.

Joe had more time to contemplate his even more uncertain future when a letter arrived from the Michigan lawyer. It's not much, but Shell Oil would like to lease the mineral rights to the now deserted farm. Why not salvage a few pennies? Of course Shell strikes oil with the first rig. Poor Joe didn't get to shelter any income from taxes, but every month a very nice check still arrives from the very nice oil company.

Joseph Kotler decided not to retire. He is now a practicing attorney, consultant to major corporations on broadcasting, and chairman of the board of Resource Development Corporation, dedicated to allowing no client to buy beef fleet of hoof—unless of course there's gold under them thar hooves.

And Bill Noe is now president of Resource Development Corporation. The company is still seeking out good tax-shel-

tered investments for its clients. After all the changes in the
tax laws, franchising and real estate still offer the best opportunities. Bill and his fellow officers are even looking into the
world fertilizer market. Knowing Bill, I'd guess they'll come
up smelling like roses.

THERE'S NO ACCOUNTING
FOR PRINCIPLES

Not everything that happened in the 1930s was bad. That was the decade in which the small investor, wiped out though he may have been in the Great Crash, began to get some protection. Richard L. Whitney, five times president of the New York Stock Exchange, went to jail for grand larceny; securities acts were passed by the Congress in 1933 and 1934; the Securities and Exchange Commission was established.

And in 1932 the American Institute of Accountants recommended that the financial statements of all public companies listed on the New York Stock Exchange be prepared in accordance with accepted principles of accounting. History does not record whether the suggestion was made in the interests of investor protection or to further establish and promote the accounting profession. Whatever the intent, GAAP (Generally Accepted Accounting Principles) was born, and like so many children, it has grown to enrich and haunt the accounting profession.

As GAAP grew, the accounting profession flourished. That little letter signed by a certified public accounting firm became the sine qua non for annual reports. "These financial statements were prepared in accordance with generally accepted accounting principles." Good principles or bad, principles that exposed, or helped to conceal, the highlights in big print and the problems in footnotes—generally accepted accounting principles, determined and set forth by accountants.

As a group, accountants are clever. GAAP, as they established them, meant reporting of the facts; it did not necessarily include responsibilities: the responsibility to check, the responsibility to question, the responsibility to report in the *worst* light. After all, accountants didn't exactly feature themselves as altruistic defenders of the faith. They were business people, and their clients were the corporations they serviced and upon whose fees they depended. Their reports were meant to enlighten the public, but it was management that paid for lunch.

The bomb dropped in 1964. The case involved the Continental Vending Machine Corporation. Three CPAs of a major accounting firm were brought to trial in a criminal proceeding. The financial position of Continental as of September 30, 1962, had been presented in accordance with "generally accepted . . ." But the court was asked to decide whether it had been *fairly* presented. The profession had bought more than it bargained for. The jury ruled that accountants had to report responsibly, not as responsible citizens but as responsible professionals. Fair disclosure and full disclosure were no longer one and the same. Guilty!

Accounting does not relate to absolute truth. It is a system of measurement that is plagued by the existence of alternative ways to measure. Accounting principles are man-made, not derived from basic axioms like the principles of the physical sciences. They are measurement compromises that have been worked out by interested parties; they are not the sole province of accountants, but they are influenced to varying degrees by management and government agencies. In many cases they involve compromises in the way that politics involves compromises. The power of the various interested parties will determine the process to be adopted in accounting rules.

Accounting is also an art, subject to interpretation, and all artists are granted some license. Corporations now pay accountants billions of dollars a year to paint their financial portraits.

Good artists know tricks to make their subjects look better. They can also use the same tricks to make a subject look worse. Sometimes worse is better.

In 1973 the Arab oil embargo gave Nixon a chance to repay some political debts. Rather than impose rationing on domestic oil supplies (as so many other countries did), our president, in a period of wage and price controls, allowed American oil producers to raise the price of their product. By year's end Exxon, Texaco, and the rest were overflowing with windfall profits. Terrific for the stockholders, but not so terrific for a public lined up at gas stations outdoors and thermostatically controlled indoors. The giants didn't dare show how much money they made. Call in the artists!

Oil companies maintain large oil reserves. In inflationary times oil at the bottom of the barrel will have cost less to produce than the new stuff currently flowing in. (Higher wages and more expensive rigs increase production costs.) In the liquid inventory from which sales were made in 1973, there was only one kind of oil, but it was oil that had come in at various times and at various costs. Now, oil doesn't spoil, and customers don't know or care whether the oil they buy was refined last month or last year. But how to account for the sales of oil on the books of Texaco? There are two accounting methods for valuing inventory, FIFO and LIFO. FIFO, "first in, first out," means that the oldest (and cheapest) oil is sold, which at current high prices means big profits. LIFO, "last in, first out," means that the more expensive new oil is sold first, which results in smaller profits. The year 1973 was no time to flaunt an oil company's riches. So that was the year the accountants changed the way inventories were evaluated, thereby managing to make it look as though the big oil companies made less money than they really did. The published figures were still embarrassingly high, but they weren't as bad (good?) as they could have been.

But—wonder of wonders—while the published figures were being lowered, the actual cash flows to the company were increased because Texaco, using LIFO, reported higher costs to the IRS and therefore paid lower taxes.

Dare one ask why the managements of many companies continue to use FIFO reporting and pay higher taxes? And why Texaco waited until 1973 to elect to report lower income and pay lower taxes? If there is a significant economic benefit in saving or deferring income taxes, why haven't more companies adopted LIFO? One reason springs to mind: the measure of management performance would be less favorable if the firm switched to the LIFO method during periods of rising prices because income would appear to be lower under LIFO. Who said less is more?

Some years ago Allegheny Ludlum Steel Corporation did the reverse: it sought permission from the IRS to discontinue using the LIFO method of valuing inventory. In addition to boosting Allegheny Ludlum's net income by $6,150,000, the change would substantially increase its tax load. Apparently the company didn't care about taxes. It wanted to report a higher paper profit in order to ward off a takeover attempt— or at least to make a takeover more expensive.

Technicalities make this kind of GAAP perfectly legal, just so long as you don't keep changing back and forth each year. But you can see how it might tend to mislead the public. There's nothing we can do about that—at least not until accounting becomes a science. But sometimes account artists have gone too far and sharp-penciled themselves into tight little corners. In some cases the law has stepped in and drawn bars around those corners. On occasion accounting firms have even been forced to compensate investors for losses suffered as a result of the CPAs' malfunction.

Bernie Cornfeld, erstwhile head of Investors Overseas Services, the Swiss-based mutual fund empire that was eventually looted of some $224 million by Robert Vesco, tried a deal of his own in 1970. And Arthur Andersen & Co., the auditors of IOS, went along with it—for a while.

In 1969 IOS officials had been telling everyone—salespeople, stockholders, potential investors, security analysts—how much money IOS was going to make that year. The most oft quoted figure was $30 million. And was it oft! It turned out that the company had been spending quite freely, what with a private jet and castle and other money-eating propositions. Talk may be cheap, but the figures weren't going to look too hot. And IOS had just gone public. What would happen to the stock—and more important, to the morale of the more than twenty thousand salespeople who had gobbled it up? The company needed an ice pack bad!

That's just what it got. Years before, one of the funds that IOS managed had bought a chunk of land in the Canadian Arctic. It was purchased for $11 million on spec when the oil people started looking around up there. And some oil had been found, not under IOS's ice but nearby. No matter; IOS still revalued the land that was sitting on its fund's books, revalued it upward by some $100 million. Consequently, the IOS-controlled fund paid to IOS (now a publicly held company) additional fees of $10 million—fees that were based solely on the sleight-of-hand increase in the fund portfolio's value. These guys simply changed the books, showed a big gain, and transferred $10 million of the fund shareholders' real dollars to the management company. In exchange, the fund got a bookkeeping entry that said it was now worth $90 million more than it had been worth a moment before.

IOS engaged in some pretty fancy maneuvering to keep its auditors off the scent. It secretly arranged to sell a small portion of the land to a group of friends for $15 an acre—land that had just been valued by independent geologists at $1.88 an acre. Then, by putting the $15 figure on all the acres, it got its $100 million valuation. Funny how a firm of the stature of Arthur Andersen & Co. couldn't see through it.

Even with the revaluation, IOS announced sheepishly at year's end that it had made only $17 million. The price of the stock began to fall. By the time the audited reports appeared in the spring, the company was bankrupt, Cornfeld was out, and the board of directors (which included a Roosevelt and a member of the Swedish royal family) was looking for someone to save what was left. When the Rothschilds withdrew their bid, Robert Vesco offered to pump $5 million into the company to keep it going. Instead of going, it went. And if the law doesn't catch up with him soon, Vesco's looted $224 million return on a $5 million investment may go down in history as one of the greatest magic acts ever.

It is impossible to tell how many financial statements are still subtly misleading the public. But enough certified public accountants are now doing time to make the rest of them nervous and cautious. (This chapter is dedicated to those who were not cautious enough.)

An honest accountant will not sign a financial statement that he deems false or misleading. But if that financial statement is issued without his signature, need he broadcast his beliefs to the appropriate authorities? Peat, Marwick, Mitchell & Co. didn't. It cost them at least $650,000.

Since 1960 Peat, Marwick, Mitchell & Co., one of the "big eight" accounting firms, had been the outside auditor for Yale Express Co. In March 1964 the Peat partner in charge of the audit certified that profits for 1963 were $1.8 million. The president of Yale Express was not thrilled; he had announced publicly a $4 million profit. He asked the auditors to check again. They did, more thoroughly this time, and they found discrepancies; even the $1.8 million figure seemed too high. They also discovered that a proposed but unaudited report, showing a $273,000 profit for the first quarter of 1964, was misleading (a loss of somewhat more than $1 million would have been about right).

The certified 1963 report went out; Peat Marwick's auditors hadn't found the discrepancies in time. The president of Yale Express also issued an unaudited six-month report for 1964 that showed profits of $717,000 (Peat Marwick's figures showed a loss of $1,012,000). But Peat Marwick did not publicly retract its 1963 certification, nor did it publicly accuse Yale's president of lying about 1964. Might we wonder whether Peat Marwick would have lost the account if it had done so?

Finally the word got out. Peat, Marwick, Mitchell & Co.

was named in a class action suit. Ultimately Peat Marwick settled out of court, making a contribution of $650,000 to a pool
for the group of plaintiffs.

Peat Marwick made news again in a case involving National
Student Marketing Corporation, a well-detailed fraud to which
NSM's president and two executive officers had pleaded guilty.
A grand jury charged that in September 1969 a Peat Marwick
partner, Anthony M. Natelli, and a member of his staff, Joseph
Seansaroli, had, as independent auditors for NSM, made unlaw-
ful, willful, and knowingly false statements with respect to an
NSM proxy statement dated September 27, 1969. According
to the *Wall Street Journal,* Cortes W. Randall, president of
NSM, when "confronted with a loss, apparently had a habit
of springing new commitments on the accounting people."

The government charged not only that "the accounting method was dubious" but that "Mr. Natelli allowed NSM to count
commitments for which written assurances never existed. In
October 1968 . . . when . . . Mr. Randall [was given] prelimi-
nary figures showing a loss for the year ended the previous
August, the company president asserted that its account execu-
tives had commitments the accounting department didn't
know about."

By some sleight of hand the company found an additional
$1.7 million in commitments to show the auditors. These com-
mitments (orders) were not supported by contracts, commit-
ment letters, or billings. No costs were charged against the
projects. The auditors didn't check as carefully as they might
have. According to the allegation, those unbilled receivables
made up $670,000 of NSM's $699,000 pretax profit for 1968.

The grand jury said the independent auditors had discovered
that of about $5 million in sales and contracts reported for
1968, some $1 million worth simply did not exist. According
to the grand jury, when the auditors recast NSM's 1968 finan-
cials for the purpose of the proxy statement, they simply camou-
flaged those nonexistent contracts.

The conviction of both men was upheld on appeal.

Price Waterhouse got off easier. In 1971 it had been the

outside auditor for DCL Inc., a computer-leasing company. In December 1971 Price Waterhouse announced to DCL management that it intended to *qualify* its certification of DCL's financial statements because it was uncertain of the company's ability to recover the cost of computer equipment through new leases and lease renewals. DCL fired Price Waterhouse.

In February 1972, while Price Waterhouse was still its official independent auditor, DCL issued the unaudited income data. Price Waterhouse apparently felt no obligation to tell anyone anything.

When the real figures came out and proved to be lower, as Price Waterhouse had expected, the price of DCL stock tumbled. In the suit that followed, the plaintiff (a stockholder holding an empty bag) alleged that Price Waterhouse knew something he didn't know and should have said something. The judge didn't agree. Silence had again become golden. Price Waterhouse must have read somewhere that good guys finish last. True, investors in DCL might not have been any better off if the truth had come out sooner rather than later. But think how much more faith we would have in that independent accounting firm that counts the ballots for the Academy Awards. No Oscar to Price Waterhouse for this one.

Early in 1970 Tally Corporation entered into serious merger discussions with General Time Corporation. The terms of the merger would depend largely on Tally's earnings in 1969 and the level of earnings that could be expected in 1970. Those earnings would determine the price that General Time (and its shareholders) would be willing to pay for Tally.

According to the SEC complaint, Tally decided to put its best foot forward. The fact that Tally didn't have a leg to stand on apparently didn't disturb the company or its auditors.

Tally is alleged to have used a "percentage of completion" accounting method to report higher revenue and profits for 1969. Under percentage of completion accounting, revenues are recognized and income is reported as the job progresses, in accordance with the amount of work done. Work is measured by the ratio of actual cost so far to total expected cost of the project. If somehow future costs can be prepaid in a current year, estimates of the amount of work completed may be increased, thereby increasing revenues and profits. Further, if the ratio of profit to cost is *estimated* at a higher amount, the percentage of profit of each dollar of cost will be estimated at a higher amount. Thus there will be higher total profits.

The juggling was complicated. According to the SEC, the "expected" 1970 sales were grossly and knowingly misprojected—misprojected by about $100 million. And in May 1970 that overstatement made Tally look about $9.2 million richer than it actually was. On May 14, 1970, Tally merged with General Time. General Time shareholders bought and paid for an additional $9.2 million that had been created out of air. Will miracles never cease?

Western Union needed a miracle in 1973. It was in trouble. Earnings per share had fallen from $2.47 in 1972 to 38 cents in 1973—not exactly a figure to gladden the hearts of stockholders or make the company attractive to prospective investors. What to do? Western Union found the answer. It had outstanding a bunch of convertible bonds that paid 5¼ percent interest. But in 1973 interest rates had zoomed up, reducing the current market value of those 5¼ percent bonds. Western Union issued new bonds carrying a 10¾ percent coupon and exchanged the new bonds for the old ones. It picked up $62 million in old bonds for $41 million in new bonds, thereby giving itself a bookkeeping profit of $21 million. The gain was legal, but it was an extraordinary gain, one unrelated to Western Union's business and not likely to recur.

That $21 million raised Western Union's per share earnings in 1973 by $1.51, from 38 cents to $1.89. The figure wasn't as good as the previous year's $2.47, but then 1973 was a bad year all around and $1.89 appeared respectable—unless the investor looked closely. Remember, the $1.89 was real; but if your broker recommended that you buy the stock based on its expected earnings increases, those increases would have had to come from a $0.38 base, not from a base of $1.89.

The category "extraordinary items" hides a multitude of sins.

Too many investors look only at the bottom line. Unfortunately, most brokers who advise those investors are neither CPAs nor even security analysts. In 1973 a lot of brokers, too, looked only at the bottom line. With a little cosmetic surgery, silk purses are still easy enough to make.

In all fairness to the accounting profession, it must be said that Western Union's extraordinary gain of $21 million was reported in its financial statements, and stockbrokers who recommended the purchase of the company's stock must accept a large measure of the responsibility if they failed to recognize the importance of the entry. To be sure, they would have had less trouble if the bottom line had read

earnings per share	$0.38
extraordinary item (per share)	1.51
earnings per share with extraordinary item	1.89

This leads us to a related area that I believe to be damaging to the credibility of accounting firms in general and the profession as a whole. In the trade the area is called materiality. And here the profession must hear our best Bronx cheer.

Accounting, we said, is not a science. Independent auditors must deal with reams of material for each company they audit. If the accountants had to highlight and explain every action a company took, financial statements could run to hundreds of pages. Therefore, accountants use their judgment with respect to which actions "materially" affect earnings and which do not. Those actions that are deemed material are explained (as in the case of Western Union); the rest are buried in the figures.

The problem is that there is no clear standard by which one may determine what constitutes a material change. According to the Accounting Principles Board (the predecessor of the Financial Accounting Standards Board), any action by a company that has an impact on earnings of less than 3 percent need not be explained; it is immaterial. The American Institute of Certified Public Accountants has recommended that 5 percent should be used as the benchmark. And Arthur Andersen

& Co. is on record as stating that in certain instances accounting changes that cause anything less than a 10 percent difference in earnings are immaterial and need not be disclosed. Well, 10 percent may not be material to the likes of Arthur Andersen, but it sure can make a hell of a big difference to an investor. Imagine, if you will, how one might feel about some mythical company whose earnings increased year after year by 5 percent and then one year it didn't do so well and its earnings just remained static. We might not be interested in buying that company's stock. But if an undisclosed accounting change could be made that showed that the company had continued to grow by 5 percent, we might think differently. Yet the profession could say that the change was immaterial—to them perhaps, but not to you and me.

A few examples may help to show some of the games accountants have tried to play and get away with for the sake of their paying clients and without regard to any impact upon investors.

In 1971 the stock of Mattel Corporation, the toy maker, was selling at a high price-earnings ratio. In prior years its earnings had been growing substantially, and investors were willing to pay a high price for the stock in anticipation of further earnings increases. Even a mild decrease in the rate of earnings growth could have caused the stock price to fall significantly.

Mattel reported record earnings for 1970. It had been a good year, and the earnings figure was determined after a $2.5 million contribution to the company's employee profit-sharing plan had been made. In 1971 the company's pretax earnings increased by $5.3 million, but the company decided not to make a contribution to its employee profit-sharing plan that year. If it had made the same contribution it had made the year before, the $5.3 million increase would have been reduced to a more consistent $2.8 million increase. While $2.8 million was certainly acceptable, it would not have had anywhere near the impact on the stock that the $5.3 million figure had. Nevertheless, the independent auditor did not deem the noncontribution of $2.5 million "material" and therefore did not disclose the nonpayment. The change in contribution *was* disclosed in the company's financial statements filed with the SEC on form 10-K, but it was omitted from the 1971 annual report to the shareholders. Does that sound like a cover-up to you? Or does it sound like one more way in which accounting firms accommodate the clients who hire them?

A much more material cover-up was perpetrated in 1969 by General Dynamics with the help, once again, of Arthur Andersen & Co. In 1969 General Dynamics reported sales of $2.5 billion and income after taxes of only $2.5 million. Not a very good showing. But the situation was even worse. That year the company's Resource Group changed its method of depreciation from accelerated to straight-line, thereby adding $5.8 million to General Dynamics' aftertax income. The auditors didn't report the change. Nor did they report that the company's Stromberg DatagraphiX subsidiary changed its accounting procedures so as to expense rather than defer start-up costs. This reduced the company's income by $6.7 million. Both changes may have been expected to result in higher certified earnings in future years. But since their combined effect on 1969 earnings was only $900,000, neither of the accounting changes nor their expected impact was reported. And it would have been close to impossible for even an accountant, much less an investor to discover the unreported changes. Need I repeat, not material to whom?

One more little example. In 1969 IT&T reported earnings of $2.90 per share, up from $2.62 the year before. What was "immaterial" (and therefore not reported) was that 9½ cents of the 28 cents increase resulted from the sales of a shopping center, a foreign plant, and foreign-held securities. The 9½ cents amounted to only 3.3 percent of the company's total per share earnings, so it was deemed immaterial. But that 9½ cents also represented 34 percent of IT&T's earnings increase. And that's damned material to an investor! The independent auditors, again, were Arthur Andersen & Co. It seems to me that these are little frauds (is that too strong a word?) the entire profession uniformly commits. And while the accounting pro-

fession and the SEC fiddle around with some concept of generally accepted principles, the investor continues to get burned.

And then there was Equity Funding. Books have been written about that scandal. Some have called it the greatest single
fraud in the history of the United States. When it was all over,
shareholders got back 12 cents on the dollar and the chief
executive officer went to jail. Private litigations have been settled for upward of $50 million. What makes Equity Funding
interesting here is that most of that $50 million came out of
the pockets of Equity Funding's outside auditors and underwriters.

While it is debatable whether Equity Funding can boast
of being the greatest fraud this country has seen, it is not debatable that it resulted in the greatest public hanging of several
very well-respected members of the accounting profession. The
fact that the accountants had to pay leads us to one of two
inescapable conclusions: either the accountants were in com-
plicity in the fraud or they were simply too stupid, too inept,
or too unprofessional to discover what had been going on for
years under their noses. In either case, they remain the people
we rely on to certify statements that become the basis for our
investment decisions. And the amount of the settlement, after
lawyers' fees, hardly began to repay investor losses.

What made the Equity Funding case so spectacular was the
nonchalance with which the hoax was perpetrated. Nearly one
hundred people within the company seem to have participated
in it or to have known about it. And the word never leaked
out, at least not until the company saw fit to fire Ronald Secrist,
an employee who knew the story. And just for spite, Secrist
called Raymond Dirks, a security analyst close to the company,
and spilled the beans.

Equity Funding went public in 1964; New York Securities
Co. underwrote 100,000 shares at $6 per share. Management
knew that stock prices go up if earnings go up. So they decided
to make earnings go up.

In 1964 the company added $361,984.97 to commission in-
come. It just made up the number. And that's how it all started.

In later years the chief executive officer would simply give the treasurer the figure he wanted for the year's earnings. The treasurer was to make any bookkeeping and computer entries necessary to create the desired figure.

The firm did some catchy things. It borrowed money and forgot to report that it owed it (about $20 million by the end of 1969). It just reported this money as income and fixed the books accordingly. The trustee's reports state that the company added a fictitious $400,000 to income in 1964. Since that worked, it kept on doing it. In 1972 alone it added a round $21 million to earnings. That certainly looked good on paper. And since no one outside the company seemed to know what was going on, and the accountants certified that it was true, it did wonders for the stock price.

When the game was over, it turned out that Equity Funding had reported, as of December 31, 1971, cash and short-term investments of $39,593,000. It was off by $20 million. As of December 31, 1972, a subsidiary reported bonds owned as assets in the amount of $24,566,791. That figure was off by more than $23 million. Yet each year the firm's independent outside auditors, the certified public accountants, using their generally accepted accounting principles, failed to see anything amiss. It's no wonder that the cost of malpractice insurance for accountants is beginning to approach that of malpractice insurance for doctors.

Equity Funding wrote insurance policies, among them 64,000 fictitious policies whose face value exceeded $2 billion. It then resold the policies to other insurance companies for cash. In the trade the process is known as reinsuring. Each year Equity Funding projected the amount of insurance it would sell, and it always exceeded its target. (Not difficult to do if you just make up the policies.) But the more it made up one year, the more it would have to make up the next. And that is what it continued to do.

The reliance that the financial world places on independent accounting reports and certifications gives CPAs enormous power to control our investment lives. Like doctors, when they give bad reports about something we like, we question them closely and sometimes even ask for other opinions. But we (investors, brokers, fund managers, etc.) are all delighted with good news. And if good news means increases in stock prices, why rock the boat?

For Equity Funding, the accounting statements meant that every public pronouncement about the company issued by Stanley Goldblum, president, and Michael Riordan, chairman of the board, rang true. The fact that Equity Funding's earnings growth defied the imagination led not to questions from analysts or brokers but rather to pats on the back for being so smart as to be in on a good thing. That Equity Funding's growth never slowed when all other companies doing similar business were affected by the vicissitudes of economic activity apparently drew no questions and raised no eyebrows.

There were clues to what was going on, but they were so widely scattered that no two pieces of the puzzle ever came together. In April 1969 Stanley Goldblum (who went to jail) and Michael Riordan (who died before the scandal was uncovered, unfortunately—but perhaps metaphorically—in a mudslide) needed a shell to cover one part of the fraud. At that time Bernie Cornfeld was divesting IOS of its American assets. One of them was Investors Planning Corporation of America, which had 29 offices and more than 2,000 sales representatives—perfect for Equity Funding's needs.

Cornfeld's chief financial officer met with Goldblum and Riordan in Geneva. He had decided that IPC was worth $5 million. So he asked $10 million, prepared to bargain down to his realistic estimate of worth. Equity Funding countered with an offer of $10.2 million. No misprint. The man from Geneva said thanks and wondered how such dumb businessmen could run so successful an operation. But that was 1969, and Equity Funding still had four years to go.

Some people did raise questions. Some remembered the story of the emperor's new clothes and even dared to mention it. The man from Geneva had no reason to question his good fortune in selling his company to Equity Funding. But my friend Arthur did have reason to question some too good Equity Funding fortune that came his way. And, as in the story of the emperor's new clothes, no one would listen.

In 1972 Arthur was a broker and portfolio manager with a New York brokerage firm. The firm was big on Equity Funding. It recommended the stock to all its clients, and many of its clients were in. Certainly all of Arthur's clients were. One day, one of his big institutional clients called with an order for 25,000 shares. Now, even with Equity Funding, a 25,000 share order sent to the floor of the New York Stock Exchange could move the stock price up several points. Arthur tried to find someone with a block of stock to sell, someone who was willing to sell at the current market price. Then, at a prearranged time, his order to buy 25,000 shares would be sent to the Exchange floor to meet the 25,000 share sell order. That's the way you do business with large blocks—so as not to disturb the market. Arthur would get a commission for buying the block, and the seller's broker would get a commission for selling it.

So Arthur went on a search. Since he had done a good deal of business in Equity's stock, he had come to know Goldblum and Riordan. It seemed only logical to call Goldblum. Perhaps he would know a potential seller. The call went to Los Angeles only to find that Goldblum was at an investment banker's office in New York. Another call, and Goldblum was on the line. After hellos and how are yous, Goldblum put the investment banker on. Arthur mentioned the block he wanted, and the banker said he did indeed know a seller.

Then a strange thing happened. The investment banker said that he would arrange for the stock to be delivered to Arthur, but he didn't want it crossed on the Exchange. However, Arthur could act as broker for both sides, the buyer and the seller. Since those were the days of nonnegotiated commissions, each side of the transaction was worth about $4,700 to the broker. Why should that guy be so nice? A bottle of wine maybe, or even a case, but $4,700? And why didn't he want the transaction to show?

Arthur said thanks but no thanks. "You take yours, I'll take mine." In that case, the banker said, he'd have the stock in about a month. Arthur hung up. Strange things happen in Wall Street, but this was one of Equity Funding's own investment bankers—and Goldblum was right there. It smelled.

Arthur went to his firm's managing partner. He told him that something was wrong with the stock most highly touted by the firm. If Arthur was right (he knew he was, but he didn't know why), the firm and its customers were in big trouble. Hear no evil, see no evil; the partner wondered whether Arthur had been smoking something illegal. After all, there were all those certified accounting statements. So Arthur returned to his desk, called all his clients, and sold them out of Equity Funding. Then he found a box, packed up the contents of his desk, and quit the firm.

For another six months Equity Funding stock kept going up. Then the emperor was exposed as exposed. Arthur's old Wall Street firm and its partners were so heavily invested on their own account that when Equity Funding died, the firm died too. (I wonder whether that partner ever thinks about Arthur anymore.)

My friend couldn't have challenged Equity Funding by himself or gone to the newspapers with his unsubstantiated feelings. There are libel laws against that. His firm however could have asked its insurance analyst to look a little more closely, just to be sure. But when a recommended stock is going up, who cares? No one seemed to. Perhaps in the back of the firm's collective mind was the belief that if there were indeed any trouble, no investor could sue it. After all, in its recommendations the firm had relied on certified financial statements.

There is one sad irony in the Equity Funding case. The auditors for the company were a small Los Angeles–based CPA firm, Wolfson Weiner. They had been with Equity Funding for years and had grown with their largest account. In 1971 the prestigious firm of Seidman & Seidman, probably eyeing the big Equity Funding account, combined Wolfson Weiner into its practice. But the same people continued to do the Equity Funding audit. Unfortunately, for those last two glorious years the reports came out under the imprimatur and responsibility of Seidman & Seidman—and Seidman & Seidman bought it!

Playing around with numbers has been going on for so long that it's almost the accepted thing to do. We know the government does it, we know the taxpayer does it. Yet it comes as a surprise, even to me, each time I discover again that some of our most prestigious and respected institutions do it too. In this instance I cite Citicorp, the bank holding company that owns Citibank, one of the ten largest banks in the country. Citicorp was trying to pull a fast one. The *New York Times* caught on; but Citicorp may get away with it nonetheless. Here's how it goes (or is going):

Banks don't get their money from depositors alone; they need capital of their own. Beyond the initial contributions of capital from the bank's organizers, most banks raise capital by selling either stock (equity) or bonds (debt) to the public. It is an accepted rule of thumb in banking that debt should not exceed 50 percent of the bank's equity. (Again, this has nothing to do with deposit money, which is subject to other rules and ratios.) If debt becomes a larger proportion of its capitalization, the bank has a problem. Prospective bondholders will not be so anxious as they might be to lend the bank money. They might even demand higher rates of interest. And as we all know, banks prefer to charge, not pay, interest.

According to Citicorp's 1978 annual report, its debt amounted to 91.6 percent of equity. Now that's pushing it a bit. Citicorp is a good company, it makes a lot of money, and no one is suggesting that it won't be able to pay the interest on its bonds or repay the principal when it comes due—but 91.6 percent for an industry that uses 50 percent as a standard?

Citicorp wants to raise more money for further expansion. It is talking millions of dollars. The alternative to bonds is to sell more stock. That would be prudent, since more equity money would lower that 91.6 percentage figure. But the stock market hasn't been kind to Citicorp common, which has been selling at a rather low price. Citicorp would prefer to issue new stock at a higher, not a lower, price, so that idea is out. That leaves new bonds. But Citicorp doesn't dare issue new bonds, considering the current debt load it is carrying.

Solution? Change the figures. And that's just what Citicorp proposes. We all know that money you owe is money you owe, whether you have to pay it back next week, next year, or fifteen years from now. Yet Citicorp has the effrontery to suggest that any debt that comes due more than fifteen years from now shouldn't be called debt at all. According to Donald S. Howard, Citicorp senior vice president and treasurer, speaking before the Ninth Annual Banking Symposium of the Financial Analysts Federation, "long-term *debt of 15 years or longer original maturity could properly be regarded as augmenting equity* to form our capital base."

What exactly is Mr. Howard trying to do? He is trying to make more than $1 billion of debt disappear. If he gets away with it, Citicorp will be able to rewrite its debt to equity ratio and proclaim to all unwitting investors (bond investors, those who count safety more highly than interest) that its debt is only 34 percent of equity. And if Citicorp says 34 percent, wouldn't you believe it? After all, if you can't trust a bank, whom can you trust?

Turning away from fraud and deceit, the issue of Generally Accepted Accounting Principles still remains. And so long as it does, investors must either be expert in the analysis of financial statements or able to find experts to do the necessary analysis to determine the actual financial position of a company in which they may be considering an investment. Very few such experts exist; most are partners of accounting firms, a few are security analysts, virtually none is a broker.

The lines have been drawn between the accounting firms (notably the "big eight") and the SEC. The accounting firms want the profession to set its own standards and to be its own policeman (look how well it has done in the past); the SEC wants real uniformity of accounting practices.

In 1973 the Financial Accounting Standards Board succeeded the Accounting Principles Board, an arm of the American Institute of Certified Public Accountants that had been widely criticized as impotent in dealing with the excesses in the profession that surfaced during the late 1960s. The FASB is composed of accountants from public accounting firms, schools, and private industry. It functions as a private body whose professional edicts are subject to the overview of the Securities and Exchange Commission. So far, so good; the SEC seems to be taking its protective role seriously.

While the FASB is supported in principle by the profession, most accounting firms fear that the presence of the SEC will whittle away their powers to audit a company in the manner that they, the accountants, see fit. They don't have to worry. In 1978 the FASB recommended a new, uniform method for certain oil and gas company accounting procedures. Surprisingly—alarmingly—the SEC overturned the FASB. Word has it that the SEC was influenced by strong political pressure from small oil companies that opposed the FASB rule for a "successful efforts" method rather than a "full cost" method of accounting.

Now the SEC has decided to study the question of accounting standards itself. The SEC estimates it will take at least three years to complete the study. And we are supposed to wait!

Meanwhile, we can all return to school to become experts in the analysis of financial statements. Or we can sit back and wonder whether certified public accountants are presenting financial data in a manner designed to enlighten stockholders or in one designed to present in the best possible posture the corporate managers who pay for lunch. There is certainly a conflict of interest here, and at present there is no indication that the conflict will be resolved in the public interest.

THE SECURITIES AND EXCHANGE OMISSION

While there can be no question that the Securities and Exchange Commission has been a force for investor protection since its establishment in 1934, there have been glaring exceptions that show up the deficiencies of the agency and expose the folly of any naive belief that because the SEC is there, all's well with your worldly goods.

The primary function of the SEC is to insure "full and fair disclosure," and its presence has certainly made corporate officials more careful about what they say and do. But not as careful as one might hope. Not as careful in the securities business because investments usually fall into grey areas. Abuses are often difficult to ascertain; to do so sometimes takes years of study, and often SEC censure is so mild as to cause little concern.

Everyone knows that New York City banks dumped New York City securities out of their own portfolios and into the hands of naive investors when New York City went through its great fiscal crisis. The banks knew about that impending crisis before the public did, and their selling took place before the public found out. But it took the SEC three years of "study" to determine that fact, and then it suggested mildly that the banks shouldn't have done it. Big deal. Not exactly Robin Hood protecting the needy.

Everyone knows that options are being abused. The SEC

is studying the problem. Accounting is a hodgepodge of misleading information; the SEC is studying the problem. Mergers that would improve investors' positions are being fought by myopic managements, using the dirtiest street tactics. And the SEC stands passively by.

In general it appears that the SEC doesn't much like tangling with the establishment, and it keeps away from the New York Stock Exchange. Left to the powers of the SEC, fixed commissions would still be with us. Rule 390, which prohibits NYSE members from trading off the floor, still is with us, even though it creates what could be called a monopoly in restraint of trade. The SEC is considering.

However, when the SEC has a grudge, it goes like hell. Bernie Cornfeld and his Investors Overseas Services defied the SEC by removing its operations from the United States and SEC jurisdiction. The SEC couldn't touch him. Arthur Lipper Corporation acted as IOS's chief broker in the United States. And made a bundle on commissions. Nothing illegal about acting as a broker for foreign corporations. Nevertheless, with Cornfeld beyond its reach, Lipper was the closest the SEC could get to him. So they pursued Lipper relentlessly, tied him up with lawyers and depositions, and tabled any attempt the firm made to register its own mutual fund. And eventually it found some small violation on which to hang him. Through Lipper the SEC got its revenge on Cornfeld.

Where the SEC really falls down, in my opinion, is in its handling of the analysts who study companies and recommend to their clients the purchase or sale of the securities offered by those companies. A good analyst knows his companies intimately and can often smell it when something is wrong. Sometimes the SEC calls using a good nose "inside information" and prevents those analysts from acting in the best interest of their clients.

Raymond Dirks was the Street's acknowledged expert on Equity Funding Corporation. He knew everyone at the company, and they knew him. He had a lot of customers who relied on his judgment and bought Equity Funding on his say-so.

Like everyone else, Ray Dirks was taken in by the fraud.

One day Equity Funding fired an employee. The employee phoned Dirks and announced that Equity Funding was a hoax. One man's word, but Dirks believed him. He called his customers and said "sell." Later the SEC said that Dirks' first responsibility was to the general public and that his first call should have been to the SEC. Dirks became a pariah to the investment community.

Perhaps Dirks was using inside information; perhaps he should not have been blindly loyal to his customers. But David MacCallum's was a different story. And it cost his firm thousands of dollars in legal fees to prove it.

David MacCallum was and is one of the best drug company analysts on Wall Street. One of the companies he studied was Bausch & Lomb.

With great hoopla Bausch & Lomb had announced a revolutionary development: the soft contact lens. The lens, if it worked, meant big profits for Bausch & Lomb. MacCallum was one of the first to recognize its potential, and he wrote it up. His customers, and those of his firm, rode up with Bausch & Lomb as the price of its stock soared.

Things looked fine for a while. Then there seemed to be problems. The soft lens wasn't working quite as well as had been expected. The company said that the problems were minor and would be resolved. MacCallum smelled trouble. He wrote an internal memorandum citing his hunches but asked his firm to withhold its publication until he had had a chance to see the vacationing Bausch & Lomb chairman. MacCallum thought that earnings for the company would be substantially lower than the Street expected. He wanted to be sure.

MacCallum called on the chairman of Bausch & Lomb. He asked a lot of questions, the same questions anyone else could have asked, and he got the same answers. Only he didn't believe them. Something wasn't right. He didn't know what it was; he didn't have any inside information. But he trusted his nose.

He called his firm from Rochester and said that it was time

to get out of Bausch & Lomb. He didn't think the company would make the money that everyone thought it would. There were lots of other companies around. He didn't need one that gave him a sinking feeling.

The head trader at MacCallum's firm began calling clients. "MacCallum is cutting his Bausch & Lomb earnings estimates. Sell!" The word was passed to the salespeople: Sell. Some salespeople were out of the office. Their secretaries were told to call their clients. Sell.

It didn't take long for the chairman of Bausch & Lomb to learn that MacCallum was cutting his earnings estimate—just a few hours. He called the firm to ask why. He didn't agree with MacCallum. "Earnings will be as high as previously reported," he said.

By 3 P.M. that same day, *after* all the firm's customers had been reached (or attempts had been made to reach them), the chairman of Bausch & Lomb telephoned again. He had consulted with his finance man. MacCallum's hunch had been right; earnings would be lower.

The following day the *Wall Street Journal* reported that MacCallum and his firm had acted on inside information! BAM!

The SEC moved in, charging a violation of the Investment Company Act regarding inside information. The SEC's case: MacCallum couldn't possibly form an *opinion* based simply on analytical expertise. MacCallum, one of the best analysts in the Street, a superstar courted by most of the top firms, couldn't form an opinion without inside information? The SEC implied that MacCallum's responsibility was to tell his firm what he thought. Then, before telling its customers (customers who paid for the firm's expertise), the firm should have confronted Bausch & Lomb, told Bausch & Lomb to confirm the "opinion," sat by until Bausch & Lomb had announced publicly that it expected to make less money than it had thought, and then—only then—should the Wall Street firm have called its customers.

Suits and countersuits were filed; the legal fees mounted. Analysts became scared to act on what they thought.

In the end the SEC said that the firm and MacCallum hadn't done anything wrong. But it added that they shouldn't do it again. That's government for you. All that time and all that money trying to demonstrate that no good deed shall go unpunished.

The Bausch & Lomb case was not an isolated instance. Nor were those sales of New York City bonds by the New York City banks. The SEC is a force for good. But too often it's at the wrong place at the wrong time, swatting at flies while the big fish keep swimming along.

If there's a moral here, it's not that "there ain't no justice." It's that you, too, have got to use your eyes and your nose. The blind belief that it can't happen to you, that the SEC is there and the crooks aren't just isn't true. *Caveat emptor* remains as valid today as it ever was.

The Penn Central case wasn't exactly the SEC's shining hour. Penn Central Transportation Co., the world's largest privately owned railroad company, with assets of over $6 billion, was an American institution ranking just behind hot dogs. On June 21, 1970, it collapsed.

Businesses had gone bankrupt before. But Penn Central stands as a glaring example of how the great institutions, the financial institutions on which we place our reliance, will get out while the getting's good and leave investors, even or especially those institutions' own clients, to get skewered. And what did the SEC do about it?

A lot of banks had lent money to Penn Central. A lot of banks had trust departments that were heavily invested in Penn Central stock. It is illegal to trade on "inside information," but when serious trouble began to show at the railroad, you can be sure that the bankers were the first to know about it—in their role not as trust officers but as lending bankers.

Ray Dirks had gotten the wind knocked out of him by the SEC when he got his customers out of Equity Funding. But what happend to Chase Manhattan Bank, Morgan Guaranty Trust, Continental Illinois National Bank & Trust, and all the others when Penn Central began to go? You bet! Their trust departments sold massive amounts of the company's stock. Put it out on the market for us investors to buy up.

There had been some talk circulating in the Street about difficulties with Penn Central. Nothing serious. But these banks *unloaded*. As for the SEC. Once again it studied. Its conclusions: "Although at this point serious questions exist about whether sales were made on inside information, it should be noted that proof of insider trading is always difficult. The difficulty is increased where, as here, there is some public adverse information which might explain the trade. Unless direct testimony or documents can be obtained on the use of inside information, it is difficult to sustain a charge of misuse of information."

And then the SEC added: "Both the commercial lending departments of Morgan and Continental had inside information at the time the trust department was selling Penn Central stock, but the parties to the decision to sell deny under oath that the trust department had access to the information."

Well, if the SEC couldn't prove anything, I'm not going to try. But who needs to? Does anyone really believe that the second floor doesn't speak to the third floor? That vice presidents don't lunch together? That secretaries don't have their pipeline? Perhaps the SEC should hire Woodward and Bernstein. Then again, it was the banks, and obviously they are above it all. As for me, I'll probably never be able to get a personal loan again.

Goldman Sachs seemed to be above it all, too. Gustave Levy, who headed the firm until his death, had at one time been chairman of the New York Stock Exchange and was held in awe by almost everyone in the investment community, including the SEC. It probably didn't hurt that Henry Fowler, former secretary of the Treasury, was then chairman of Goldman Sachs' international operations.

Goldman Sachs had dominated the commercial paper market for generations. Commercial paper is issued by the best corporations in America to raise quick cash. These unsecured promissory notes are usually issued for a term of ninety days, and they are considered by most sophisticated investors to be every bit as good as short-term U.S. Treasury bills. And they pay a higher rate of interest.

The National Credit Office rates commercial paper. Only the highest grade can be widely offered. On February 5, 1970, an official of NCO became alarmed at the earnings reports published by Penn Central. He called an official at Goldman who reassured him that Penn Central's properties and security holdings were enough to offset the dismal earnings reports and that Goldman Sachs was continuing to sell the company's paper.

The official must have been persuasive. NCO retained Penn Central's prime rating, the rating that investors rely on as an independent opinion of the company's credit worthiness.

But Goldman Sachs wasn't relying on any independent outsider. It knew well enough what was going on. Business as usual for the firm's clients, but a private deal with Penn Central that it would buy back $10 million of its own commercial paper that Goldman Sachs had in its own inventory. By the time Penn Central hit the fan, Goldman Sachs did not own one dime's worth of Penn Central paper.

Goldman's customers weren't so lucky. Nor were corporations in general, for the collapse of Penn Central threw the entire commercial paper market out of whack. There followed the equivalent of a run on the banks as everyone tried to cash in the commercial paper of all firms and as corporations found that those needed short-term borrowings would have to come directly from the banks. Fortunately, the Federal Reserve stepped in to supply banks with the necessary funds to make the loans.

What happened to Goldman Sachs? It had acted on inside information. It had not disclosed that information to the public. It had saved its skin while skinning others. And the SEC? It censured Goldman Sachs. It allowed the firm to consent to the SEC action without admitting or denying the charges. The SEC said, "Don't do it again." But what help was the good old SEC to the defrauded investor? Not a whit. That's government in defense of the governed! But, as we've pointed out, former SEC members often end up in Wall Street—and you only bark at, you don't bite, the bank or broker that may someday feed you.

Fortunately, the public has recourse to the courts when all else fails. The Penn Central collapse and the debacle in the commercial paper market that followed found Goldman Sachs named in nearly fifty lawsuits.

Goldman settled with nearly half of the claimants for twenty cents on the dollar. The others held out, and most of them did better. Some even got all their money back. (Franklin National Bank lost $500,000, held out, got it all back, and then proceeded to bankrupt itself a few years later.)

In October 1974 a six-member jury found that Goldman Sachs had defrauded three of its customers of $3 million. The firm had sold them Penn Central commercial paper at a time when Goldman Sachs knew that the railroad was terminally ill. Goldman Sachs was ordered to pay back the $3 million plus about $1 million in interest. Now that's a little better than the SEC's "Don't be naughty again."

There's a lesson to be learned here. When millions of dollars are at stake, the marbled pillars of Wall Street—the banks and the most respected investment brokers—become battlements, fortresses in which the line starts forming. And they, not you, are going to be first on that line. When it's big money, it's every man for himself, and by comparison, the small investor is just a kid.

And then there's the story of New York City's finding itself on the brink of financial disaster. The SEC was a big help in that one, too.

It was December 17, 1974. The limousines pulled up one by one. Frank Smeal from Morgan Guaranty Trust; Tom Labrecque from Chase; Richard Kezer from First National City; Gedale Horowitz from Solomon Brothers; Wallace Turner from Merrill Lynch. More cars, more names. These were the bankers and underwriters, the municipal bond men. They came to breakfast with a client and to tell that client, "No more"—no more loans, no more bond issues. The client wasn't making good on its obligations. It faced default on its previously issued bonds. Enough.

The group assembled had recently syndicated a $475 million offering for the client and in the process lost $50 million among themselves. And now the client needed still more money to stay afloat. Clients like this you don't need.

But they came anyway. They came to Gracie Mansion because Abraham D. Beame, mayor of New York City, had asked them to come.

For years New York City had been spending more money than it took in. The process had begun years before Beame took office, and it had continued under him. For years the city had engaged in long-term borrowing to finance short-term debts. No corporation in America could get away with this practice, but New York City was a "municipality," and no government or government agency was subject to SEC requirements for the disclosure of financial condition before trying to raise money from the public. For years New York City had borrowed from the public on its good name. It had propagated the myth that, since New York City was the second largest government in the United States, second only to the federal government itself, New York City bonds had to be safe. If New York City went under, so would the United States. Or so went the myth.

New York was in financial trouble. Moody's and Standard and Poor's, the country's two most widely known bond-rating services, knew it. For years they had tried to tell investors. Once one of them had even lowered its rating of New York City bonds. When the news hit the press the city cried foul. It made such a fuss that the agency relented and restored New York's better name. It raised the rating, but apparently for political rather than economic reasons (or are they the same?). Yet the bankers knew what was really going on. And so did investors—sort of. New York City kept issuing bonds, but the price kept going up. The city had to pay higher and higher rates of interest to get its bonds sold. Not because the bankers were greedy but because investors knew that New York City paper wasn't as safe as it had been. No one expected the city to default. But New York City was a bigger risk than Los Angeles, and you have to be paid for risk.

And now they came for breakfast, these captains of finance. They came to say that the public was beginning to sense what they had known for months: that New York City was really in trouble, that New York City couldn't be counted on to repay its bonded debt. The myth no longer could be sold, regardless of the rate of tax-free interest it offered. The condition of New York City's finances, so long shielded by immunity to disclosure, had leaked out to the public. You can fool some of the people some of the time, and all of them had been fooled for too much time. Armageddon was at hand.

The bankers weren't talking much about how they had been selling off their own inventories of New York City bonds in recent months, selling off their own investments while continuing to offer New York City bonds to the public. They weren't talking about how they had used their intimate knowledge of New York City's finances to get out of their lousy investments by passing them on to their own unsuspecting customers. They had continued to underwrite New York City bonds, but recent issues hadn't found their way into the banks' own portfolios. They knew a bad thing when they saw it. But the new issues gave them time to dump some of their own inventories. And since the city didn't have to disclose its perilous state, the banks felt no obligation to tell the public what they knew. Besides, this was only 1974.

Not until August 26, 1977, would the SEC issue a staff report charging that Mayor Beame, City Comptroller Harrison Goldin, six New York City banks, and Merrill Lynch had *knowingly* misled investors in city securities by failing to disclose the city's perilous condition. Since those were the big boys, they only got slaps on the wrist from the SEC. The people, the small investors who trusted the banks, who felt safe dealing with the banks, had nervous breakdowns, screamed at their kids, or canceled their summer vacations. The bankers and Merrill Lynch went on with business as usual. And as usual they used their stellar reputations to keep their profits up—and the public be damned.

But on that morning in December 1974 the jig was up. The banks had thought they could do it one more time: In October 1974 they had underwritten one more bond issue—the $475 million one—but the public, at least some of the public, wasn't buying, and the banks took their $50 million licking. That was too much. They didn't much mind selling dirt that had been made to look like gold by their endorsement. But to have to take it themselves? No more!

The bankers came to say that the proposed January 1975 sale of new bonds would have to be canceled. Not the sophisticated investors, not even the unwitting public could be made to buy those bonds. New York City, Brooklyn Bridge and all, had been sold once too often.

Rumor has it that the mayor, outraged, railed against the banks. (Offense can be the best defense.) He claimed that the banks were milking the city. The last issue had gone at a tax-free 9½ percent. It was the banks' fault, not the city's. Although the city should have gone to debtors' prison, Beame blamed the banks. He threatened to get even by using the city's pension system to cut out the banks.

That was the most grievous sin. Pension funds are a sacred trust. New York City's combined pension funds then had assets approaching $9 billion, all of it earmarked for retirement benefits to past and current employees whose financial well-being depended on the proper administration of those funds. Sure, most of those funds had come from the city—not as a gift, but as part of workers' compensation. Employees had contributed a sizable portion, too. But regardless of the city's contribution, the money was no longer its own. The mayor and the comptroller were among the funds' trustees, charged with managing that money in the best interests of firemen, policemen, secretaries, and schoolteachers. Even the mayor's own retirement pension would come from those funds. That's money you don't play around with. You hire the best advisers and you invest it soundly.

In fact the city had hired the best names (Bank of New York, U.S. Trust Company, Citibank, Alliance Capital Corporation) to do just that, to decide for the trustees what portion of those funds should be held in bonds, what portion in common stocks. And now in a crisis, the mayor was threatening to counter his adversaries with the clout of $9 billion in funds entrusted to his care. He was using monies for which he was a trustee to flex his political muscle. Once upon a time we might have expected that kind of thing from the Teamsters. But from the mayor of the City of New York?

Until the early 1960s, the pension funds of New York City and New York State had been brimming with bonds issued by those state and local authorities. The pension funds were ready buyers of the safe securities. Moreover, the funds had lots of cash, and they could absorb any amount of new bonds that might overhang the municipal bond market.

Then, one day, someone realized that pension funds pay no taxes. Why then should the funds hold tax-exempt bonds that paid lower rates of interest than their AAA-rated corporate cousins? Municipal bonds may be fine for an individual in a high tax bracket, but they made no sense at all for a non-tax-paying pension fund. Why no one realized this until the 1960s is hard to fathom. But beginning in that decade, pension funds began to divest themselves of the lower yielding municipal bonds they had irresponsibly invested in for so many years. (The Employee Retirement Income Security Act of 1974 had already made corporate pension funds and their managers subject to federal scrutiny. ERISA makes those managers a little more prudent knowing the law, or at least knowing that the pension's members armed with the law, are breathing hard on their collars. But municipalities were still free from federal scrutiny.)

By the end of 1975, New York City was to repay $400 million to holders of its notes that had come due. The city announced that it would not—could not—repay those obligations. Sugarcoat the language as it might, New York City had defaulted. The largest city in the nation could not pay its bills. It applied to Washington for help, and President Ford told the city to shove it.

In this context Beame decided to use the pension funds to bail out the city—to the tune of $2.5 billion. It seemed like a nice solution—except to the people whose pensions those funds represented. The mayor was going to force the unions to bail out the city!

The police went to court. The court ruled against the city: a pension fund could not be *forced* to make investments it chose not to make. But the fund could volunteer to make investments if the trustees thought the investments were prudent ones.

Somehow the trustees were made to feel that it would be prudent to buy the city's paper. In 1975 the Employee Retirement System bought $50 million in city obligations; the teachers bought $75 million. In January 1976 the five pension funds liquidated $155.6 million of corporate securities to help the city meet its cash needs. Then came the big step: over the next three and one-half years the funds would buy a total of $2.5 billion in Municipal Assistance Corporation (Big Mac) bonds. Prudent, eh? About 30 percent of the New York City pension funds' assets invested in an entity of dubious prospects? No corporation could get away with that. Even the Teamsters in its heyday wouldn't have tried.

Some people worried that the funds might lose their tax-exempt status. Washington took care of that problem. In March 1976 the House Ways and Means Committee approved a bill exempting the New York City pension funds from a long-standing rule that a pension fund would lose its tax-exempt status if it used its investments to aid or improve an entity in which it had invested. Further, the trustees demanded and received immunity from prosecution for wrongdoing. Was this any way to manage a pension fund? They knew it wasn't.

Those hurdles out of the way, the comptroller instructed the "advisers" to the funds to start liquidating other investments and begin buying Big Mac bonds.

The "advisers" had been hired through the Comptroller's

Office after an exhaustive search; they were considered the best available. Their role was to use their financial expertise to prudently invest funds that belonged to people who had no investment competence. The "advisers" became a kind of trustee. Now they were being instructed to make investments that they knew were not prudent. They worried about that, but most of the advisers managed only the portions of the funds that were held in common stocks. Two alone, Citibank and U.S. Trust Company, managed the combined pension funds' bond holdings.

The equity advisers were instructed to sell off substantial portions of the common stock investments and deliver the proceeds to the bond advisers. The city had no problem with Citibank. Even though the immunity that covered the fund's trustees did not apply to the banks (the trustee's trustee), Citibank did as it was told and bought however many Big Mac bonds it was instructed to buy. U.S. Trust was a different story.

Hans Jepson had recently come to U.S. Trust Company from Alliance Capital Corporation. U.S. Trust primarily manages money, about $12 billion worth, and Jepson was its executive vice president and chief investment officer. He had been hired to add some life to the old institution, to revitalize it, improve its investment performance and to draw in new accounts. One of his first acts was to resign an account.

Jepson had peculiar notions about integrity. Despite the guarantees of immunity, despite the votes of trustees, the Big Mac bonds were not suitable investments for the pension funds that Jepson's group managed. U.S. Trust Company would not compromise. It lost the account.

God sometimes protects the meek. New York City did not go under, and the pension funds are getting a reasonable return on their Big Mac bonds. Abraham Beame saved the city, but in doing so he used the wrong tools; he could have gone over the brink and taken the pension funds with him. Instead the voters sent him home to live outside public politics on the very handsome pension that he had earned for his years of city service—a pension that he and hundreds of thousands of others could have lost through his financial recklessness.

The victory was not won without cost. The spectre of New York City's defaulting cast a long shadow, long enough to be seen today over the entire municipal bond market. New York City's financial mismanagement still costs the city millions each year in the higher interest costs it must pay to raise new money. And the ratings of the bond-rating agencies no longer have the blanket acceptance they once enjoyed. The investor can no longer view municipal bonds complacently or buy them with the paramount criterion of tax-free income. He now has to make sure that the bonds he buys will yield an income, tax-free or otherwise. It's time to be careful again. It's time to make sure you and your broker know something about the quality of the tax-free bond he's recommending.

But that may not be a simple matter. Municipalities, through their arcane relationship to the federal government, established through a self-serving reading of the Constitution's provision for separation of powers between state and federal governments, still do not have to report certified (or even noncertified) statements of financial condition. They don't have to tell the public anything.

For years investors have bought municipal bonds strictly on the assumption that a municipality could always repay its debt. After all, cities could raise taxes, sell their properties, or lay off workers to insure that bondholders would always be the first paid.

Well, New York City couldn't raise taxes in 1974; the public wouldn't stand for it. It couldn't raise corporate taxes; the city-based corporations threatened to pack up and move out. It couldn't raise the stock transfer tax; the New York and American stock exchanges began negotiating for space in Jersey City.

The mayor did lay off a number of seemingly superfluous city workers. But the unions howled. And the unions control votes. Certainly New York City did not attempt to sell off Central Park, probably the most valuable piece of open space in the world. It just let the bondholders swing in the breeze. And worse, a court said it was okay. A court excused New

York City from the prompt repayment of its debt. Although a higher court reversed that opinion, it remains an indication of how much your municipal bonds are worth when the chips are down.

First New York, then Cleveland. Which city will be next to discover its suddenly acute financial problems, perhaps even to make up some crisis in order to obtain federal grants or loans or to apply pressure to the unions? Which city next? It certainly couldn't be the one whose municipal bonds you hold. Could it?

Back to the banks. One of their major areas is the trust department. The big push these days is for the management of the big pension funds; that's where the money is—the big fee money. The Big Mac bonds aside, the performance of most bank-managed pension funds is dismal, and if you are part of a pension plan, it might pay you to look into its management (it's your pension, and therefore your right). You might not be able to change the system, but you might ruffle some feathers and have some fun in the process. On the average, the performance of most bank-managed pension funds during the 1970s was substantially less than that of a day of deposit, day of withdrawal savings account. And nobody, nobody who knows better, uses a 5¼ percent account when the liquid asset funds pay nearly double that.

Bank trust departments manage hundreds of billions of dollars. Most of it comes from wills that name a bank as the manager of the deceased's assets for the benefit of the heirs. After all, aren't banks safe, secure, conservative, and expert in the management of other people's monies? Who better to entrust hard-earned (or not so hard-earned) fortunes or semifortunes to? Who better indeed?

Most banks seem to be very good about handling their own money. The record shows, however, that most banks are not very good about handling yours.

I am not sure how typical is the case of my friend Stephanie. Nobody likes to talk much about it. But I have a feeling that her situation is shared by lots of others.

Stephanie was left about $200,000 when her parents died in 1970. The sum of $200,000 doesn't go down in the record books as a monumental inheritance, but it's not exactly peanuts either.

Stephanie's parents had an able lawyer. He knew how to write wills, and he knew about "grandfather trusts." If you create a grandfather trust, you effectively leave your estate to your heir's heirs. Stephanie would get the income from the trust, and in dire circumstances she could, from time to time, invade the principal. But legally the money had been left to Stephanie's children, who wouldn't get it until she died. And not until that time would estate taxes have to be paid. That's the tax shelter of grandfather trusts: you skip a generation of inheritance taxes.

Not uncommonly, a bank is named to administer a grandfather trust. In this case it was one of the better-known New York banks, one whose name brings immediate reaction. The will also stipulated that Stephanie would receive an income of $500 a month for the rest of her life, that is, $6,000 a year, or 3 percent per year of the $200,000 principal.

Banks like to manage trust accounts. They collect fees as trustees, fees as custodians, and fees as money managers. The fees are regulated by law and are not as large as banks would like them to be, and perhaps they are not as large as they ought to be to insure superior service. Yet banks in this country manage hundreds of billions of dollars in trust accounts. And those accounts, along with the bank-managed pension funds, make banks the largest institutional investing group in the nation.

Stephanie knows beans about investments. Stephanie's parents didn't know much more. The lawyer who wrote the will probably wasn't very smart either, but he knew that he couldn't get into too much trouble if he arranged the trust through a "great" New York bank. After all, a bank that manages other people's billions could certainly manage Stephanie's $200,000.

Stephanie was even proud to have this great bank managing her money. It had a certain status appeal, and she was happy to let the experts do their job. So she thought.

The important consideration here was that Stephanie receive her $500 a month. You see Stephanie wasn't married and she had no children. There was no explicit or even tacit understanding that the bank should try to make the money grow. Just make sure Stephanie got her $6,000 a year.

The bank had several choices. It could put the money into long-term bonds (very long term) and collect 7–8 percent interest on AAA corporates. That way the $200,000 would increase each year by 7–8 percent, with 3 percent being paid out to Stephanie. But she would have to pay income taxes on that $6,000 a year. Good but not great. So the bank rejected that idea.

The bank could put the money into long-term municipal bonds. The best ones were paying about 5 percent at the time; that would mean $10,000 in *tax-free* income to the trust, out of which $6,000 would be tax-free income to Stephanie. And each year the trust would grow by $4,000, an extra $4,000 that could become useful in case Stephanie ever had to invade for that possible emergency. This plan really would have made sense. But the bank didn't choose it either.

Instead the clever bank trust officer took Stephanie's money, commingled it with lots of other "small" accounts, and put it into a kind of bank-run mutual fund. After all, it's too much trouble to handle those little accounts separately—much easier to put them all together, create one big one, and give it to a trust officer to run.

And run it he did. Right into the ground. All the money was put into common stocks. And this bank wasn't a good stock picker. The last statement I saw showed that Stephanie's $200,000 had become $80,000. Stephanie is still getting her $500 a month, but most of it now is coming out of principal. One of these days, probably before Stephanie hits fifty, the trust will dry up.

Stephanie should sue. The bank was grossly negligent. But, like Scarlett, she says she'll think about it tomorrow. She doesn't even read the statements these days. She's too angry, and besides she can't really imagine not getting that monthly check in perpetuity. She also can't imagine winning a lawsuit against a bank that boasts some $10 billion in assets. And she doesn't know if Abe Pomerantz would be interested in coming to her defense and the defense of however many others are in her predicament. So Stephanie remains a passive investor. She buries her head and hopes the problem will go away.

Stephanie is a victim. By failing to exercise proper fiduciary responsibility, that bank stole her blind and is getting away with it. Funny, Stephanie is the type who never carries more than $20 in cash, just in case she should get mugged. Of course, when muggers get caught, they often go to jail. It may not be nice to talk about banks this way, but that stupid trust officer has mugged Stephanie out of $120,000—so far. And still he sits in his richly furnished office, picture of the wife and kids in a silver frame, and speaks authoritatively about the vicissitudes of the stock market and how fondly he remembers Stephanie's parents.

Would you buy a used car from that guy? If he's managing your money, that's all you may be able to afford.

In all fairness to bank trust officers and the Stephanies they manage, not all the blame can be placed in their court. Stephanie has some available alternatives that might have obviated the need to sue. For one, she could have become an "informed beneficiary," the equivalent of an informed investor.

There was a time when it seemed that only the rich used banks to handle their estates. But the definition of rich is changing. The Bank of New York advertises itself as the bank that manages money. If you have $300,000 or more, they'd like to see you. And a lot of people have estates of $300,000, and their heirs will need to have them managed. Bank trust departments have the reputation to manage them, along with the hundreds of billions of dollars entrusted to them by will-writers who hope that the banks also have the expertise to keep their heirs comfortable.

They do have the expertise, but they also have thousands of clients. Most get handled like Stephanie. But you don't have to be. If you have a trust, it's a good idea to get to talk with your trust officer. Let him know that you want to know what he's doing and why. Doesn't matter what the size of the trust is. An interested customer has to be spoken to. Find out if your money is in stocks or bonds, or both, and find out why. Maybe it's where it is only because no one has bothered to think about it. Maybe it's there because no one really knows what your needs are. And while you're at it, find out what happens with cash that happens to accumulate in your account. The bank is probably using it for its own profit.

Here's one of the truth-is-stranger-than-fiction parts of the Wall Street game. Banks can manage trust accounts or individual management accounts. Fees on IMAs are subject to negotiation. But in New York, for example, trust account fees are regulated by the State Banking Commission. Under current law a bank may charge no more than seven-tenths of one percent on the first $300,000 in a trust, and no more than three-eights of one percent on the next $500,000. You can't make a living on those figures. Bank trust departments have continually beseeched the Banking Commission to raise the rates, in part to increase their profits, but in part too to be able to provide the service that trusts deserve. The commission keeps refusing these requests. It says that the rates are high enough, particularly because it is *expected* that trust departments will use the cash balances in their customers' accounts for their own benefit; that other areas of the bank will consider those monies as part of the bank's reserves from which loans will be made or will simply invest those idle funds and collect the interest for themselves. Of course, if you tell the trust officer that you want your cash balances continually invested at interest, he will have to do that for you, just as brokers must. But most trust accounts are run for passive investors who don't bother to do that sort of thing.

What boggles my mind is that New York State can knowingly work out fees that are based in part on someone's effectively stealing someone else's money. Obviously, they don't look at it that way; but isn't that really what's happening?

Suppose, for example, that I am the treasurer of a corporation. The corporation has some money—maybe a lot of
money—sitting in a checking account. I know that checks won't
be written on that account for a week. So I use my authority
to withdraw that money, and I put it into a savings account
for a week. If it's a lot of money, the interest for a week could
be a fair bit of change. At the end of the week I put the money
back into the checking account, but I pocket the interest.

When the boss finds out what I have done, not only will I
get fired, I will go to jail for misappropriation of funds. Do
we have a double standard in this country? The state-supported
banking schemes—no, the state-*required* banking schemes—
begin to make the Mafia look silly.

Many banks, particularly the large commercial banks, seem
to like things just as they are. They even like the idea that
most of the people whose trust accounts they manage don't
bother them. Certainly Stephanie's bankers don't care to have
her nosing around and asking questions. Other bankers, however, want their customers to become "informed beneficiaries."
The term is not mine; it comes from the chief trust officer at
U.S. Trust Company. U.S. Trust wants its clients to know what's
going on. Sure, it may be able to use your inquisitiveness as
a lever to raise those allowable fees. But those fees will more
than be made up for by the interest that you, not the bank,
will get on your idle balances. And they will also go a long
way toward hiring the better people, at rates competitive with
the better firms in the biokerage industry, to give you the
service that at least one bank thinks you deserve.

One point is worth repeating: If you have or are planning
a trust, it is naive to believe that a big bank is going to do its
best job for you just because you are one of its accounts. The
bank will tell you that it will; it will say that all its accounts
are treated equally. But that's just not true. The accounts that
demand more service get it. The accounts that demand ac-
countability are not handled as cavalierly as the others. The
accounts that know enough to ask questions get answers.

Most people will say that they care about their money. Their actions indicate that they don't. Many in fact seem to think that money is really dirty and the less they know about it the better. When it comes to your money in a bank-run trust, often the less you know about your money, the less there will be to know about.

AFTER WORDS

There once was a naive young creature
Whose broker named Smith did beseech her.
She bought all his pitches
And lost all her riches.
That's not what a damn Smith should teach her!

According to Adam Smith the father (not to be confused with the son or ghost who surfaced on Wall Street in the late 1960s), the wealth of nations derived from each individual pursuing his own self-interest. The principle of laissez-faire rests upon the assumption that we all do well by doing good. I guess old Adam looked around, way back in 1776, and saw that a baker baking nice breads did okay for himself when customers kept coming back; and innkeepers who watered the scotch didn't. And he probably would have said that George III lost the Colonies because he wasn't mad about his job.

The history of Wall Street is a history of laissez-faire. Investors had always been presumed to be knowledgeable and caring enough about their savings to invest them prudently. And if they fell victim to some scam, so what? After all, to have savings at all, to be able to join in the action meant that you could afford to lose. On that assumption, governments and other regulators left the field to itself. That might have been all right if indeed only the wealthy gamed among themselves, if only the Morgans outfoxed the Vanderbilts or the Carnegies fricked

174

the Fricks. But from the great Tulip scandal to the South Sea Bubble to the Crash of 1929 the small investor has been fair game.

Laissez-faire is supposed to work in that ideal world where everyone knows the rules and everyone has alternative courses of action to follow when the game doesn't go according to plan. It may have worked on Robinson Crusoe's island, but no civilized, complex society can afford to leave its destiny to an unrestricted interaction among millions of individuals, each in pursuit of his own best interest. We may not like to think of it in these terms, but we rely upon Big Brother to watch over us. What other justification is there for the CAB or the FDA, the FDIC, or the AEC? We are more comfortable because somebody up there licenses doctors—we don't think it's a very good idea to let just anyone cut us open on the presumption that if we don't survive, word will get around and a resulting lack of patients will force the would-be healer into another profession. We seem to need some outside help to keep General Motors from doing well by polluting our air or by putting Chevy motors in Olds packages.

There is no upbeat ending for this Wall Street story. So long as Wall Street does well even if most of its customers don't, something is wrong. So long as we keep going back for more even though more may mean increasingly less, something doesn't figure.

It's hardly likely that 1929 will occur again. But that's not a guarantee. History has been known to repeat itself, and if another Great Crash came the consequences would be unthinkable. Investing today is no longer just about keeping out of the kitchen if you can't stand the heat. Today it's about those millions of pension-plan people whose lives depend upon their often unwitting participation in the market. It's about all those naive people like Dorothy Lawrence who fade away without so much as a whimper when the Street does them in. And it's about those proverbial widows and orphans who have been so carefully persuaded to respect the presumed integrity of our most sacred institutions.

Of course it's better than it used to be, out there in investor
land. Even Abe Pomerantz would grant that. It's better to
have an SEC than not. It's better to have a few people in
jail just to set an example. It's better to have some accounting
than to have no one accounting at all. But it's not enough,
and it's still every man for himself out there on the Street. If
we will stand for anything maybe Wall Street doesn't have
to change. Maybe Adam Smith was right after all. Maybe if
we weren't so eager to buy, we couldn't be so easily sold.

It's not so easy to make a million in the stock market. But
it shouldn't be so tough for so many just to keep some of the
marbles they've won. It happens a lot when you play in the
Street.

ABOUT THE AUTHOR

ALAN LECHNER began his Wall Street career as the author of *Industrial Aid Financing*, a how-to book for Wall Street insiders. He continued his financial career as a security analyst and president of Resource Programs Institute, a firm advising on tax shelters.

In 1971 he left the Street to become an independent investment adviser and professor of economics at Brooklyn College of the City University of New York.

He received his Ph.D. from New York University and lives in New York City.